EMBRACING EDITH STEIN

Wisdom for Women
from
St. Teresa Benedicta of the Cross

ANNE COSTA

SERVANT
BOOKS

PUBLISHED BY FRANCISCAN MEDIA
Cincinnati, Ohio

Cover design by Mary Ann Smith
Cover image © TomShahar | Getty Images
Book design by Mark Sullivan

LIBRARY OF CONGRESS CATALOGING-IN-PUBLICATION DATA
Costa, Anne.
Embracing Edith Stein : wisdom for women from St. Teresa Benedicta of the Cross / Anne Costa.
pages cm
Includes bibliographical references.
ISBN 978-1-61636-681-0 (alk. paper)
1. Stein, Edith, Saint, 1891-1942. 2. Christian philosophers—Germany—Biography. 3. Carmelite Nuns—Germany—Biography. 4. Christian martyrs—Germany—Biography. I. Title.
BX4705.S814C67 2014
282.092—dc23
2013041865
ISBN 978-1-61636-681-0

Published by Servant Books, an imprint of
Franciscan Media
28 W. Liberty St.
Cincinnati, OH 45202
www.FranciscanMedia.org

Printed in the United States of America.
Printed on acid-free paper.
14 15 16 17 18 5 4 3 2 1

In memory of my dear friend, Krista,
in celebration of
"Our Jewish Friend"

• contents •

Like Anne Costa, I was touched by the work of St. Teresa Benedicta of the Cross—better known to the world as Edith Stein—at a critical point in my journey. I was in my mid-twenties, doing my graduate work in theology at the John Paul II Institute for Studies on Marriage and Family. In surveying those great thinkers who influenced the teachings of John Paul II, we studied the works of Edith Stein. I remember being pierced by her insights into human nature and, in particular, by her insights into the nature and dignity of woman. I have taken those insights with me around the world in my work teaching John Paul II's Theology of the Body.

Throughout this book, we can see Edith's foundational influence on John Paul II. Both were brilliant scholars, deep thinkers, and contemporaries who shared a love for phenomenology (a modern approach to the study of reality through the careful examination of our experience of it). Nevertheless, this book is *not* a scholarly reiteration of Edith's life; instead, it is a revealing and personal story about Anne's love and admiration for a saint who profoundly touched her life. As the story of their friendship unfolds, readers will gain a deeper grasp and understanding of their own inherent dignity in light of what John Paul II called the "feminine genius."

Edith Stein understood well that right from the beginning, the Enemy of Human Nature (St. Ignatius of Loyola's preferred term for the devil) had his sights set on "the woman." Why? Summarizing insights gathered from Stein herself, John Paul II wrote that woman "is the representative and the archetype of the whole human race: she *represents the humanity* which belongs to all human beings, both men and women" (*Mulieris Dignitatem,* 4). In other words, woman teaches all of us the deepest truth of what it means to be human: to be open in order to *receive* divine love, *conceive* divine love, and *bear it forth* for others. This is the theology of a woman's body and soul. This is woman's particular genius. And *this* is why woman is so violently attacked by the Enemy: she welcomes God into the world; she gives flesh and birth to God…and the Enemy is an anti-Christ from the beginning.

Anne is absolutely right that "women today are hungry for deeper meaning in their lives" and "struggling to understand who they are called and created to be." She's also absolutely right that women today can find compelling answers to the deepest questions of their hearts by "embracing Edith Stein." May all who read this compelling work rediscover the true dignity and lofty vocation of woman and, through that, the true dignity and lofty vocation of all humanity.

—*Christopher West*

• *a c k n o w l e d g m e n t s* •

First and foremost, I would like to thank the Holy Spirit, from whom all graces and inspiration flow. He is the cause of my joy as he pours his blessings into the well-watered garden of my life! As always, I stand in awe of the fearfully and wonderfully made individuals that the good Lord has allowed to grace my path and am deeply grateful for their beautiful presence, companionship, and love.

I'd especially like to thank Kathy Kreinheder, who so lovingly and gently read this manuscript with an open heart and shared so much to help make it better: Your encouraging spirit and faithful friendship are so very special to me. I love you. And to her devoted husband Gary, who is just a great guy as far as I'm concerned!

I have to acknowledge the Heavenly Hatties who are my spiritual posse: Mary M., Alice, Katie S., Krista, Veronica, Barbara, Maria, Trudy, and of course, Edith.

To Claudia Volkman, my editor, who believed in this book and gave me the chance to turn a six-minute pitch into this manuscript that is so dear to my heart: Thank you for your support and enthusiasm.

And finally, a heartfelt thank you to my husband, Mike, and daughter, Mary, who have adjusted to the long stretches of time with Momma being holed up in her room, hunched over the keyboard. I love you guys forever.

Edith Stein is a friend of mine. Otherwise known as St. Teresa Benedicta of the Cross, she has blessed me with her words and the example of her life, providing wise counsel and speaking to my heart as profoundly as if she were sitting across my kitchen table. When I read and study her writings, I come away with a sense that I have spent time with someone who truly understands what it means to be a faithful woman in our modern times and who offers a prescription for living that feeds my soul.

I am excited to share the story of my friendship with this remarkable woman and saint through the pages of this book. Edith acted as a guide and mentor to me at one of the most confusing times of my life, during the period when I was contemplating returning to the Catholic Church after being away for a long time. When I eventually did return, I discovered her writings quite by accident—though their impact on my life was certainly no accident. From the very first word, I was drawn in by her clarity and passion on such topics as the formation of women, the feminine soul, and the role of women in Church and society. When I wasn't entirely sure if the Catholic Church would accept me back or if I would find a place to fit once I returned, Edith's words seemed to be offering me a place of affirmation and a consolation.

You may be in the same situation of coming back to the Church—or know someone who is. Or maybe you have been a Catholic for a long time, without really understanding the Church's teachings on women. No matter what you are going through in life, I am certain that you will find a nugget of knowledge or a word of wisdom from Edith. In the same way that you would consult a friend, you can turn to Edith Stein as a saintly confidant—someone you can approach for advice and intercession. If you are confused, exhausted, or anxious, Edith has some kind and hope-filled words for you. If you are seeking a saintly sister in Christ who can celebrate your victories and take your heart whispers straight to the King, she won't let you down.

Edith's own spiritual journey took her from the worldly circles of a Jewish philosopher and intellectual to the soul-rich, hidden life of Carmel following her conversion to Catholicism in 1922 and her final profession of vows in 1938. Her faith carried her toward the ultimate sacrifice, when she was taken prisoner and killed at the Auschwitz death camp in 1942. She spent the first part of her life seeking truth— and found it, in the form of a Person, Jesus Christ, through the Roman Catholic Church. She was a brilliant teacher and noted doctor of philosophy who became a humble student, a woman in love, who became a martyr.

Many of those who knew her were enriched by the acquaintance. A friend of hers from Göttingen wrote that she was always a blessing and that she was one of those people that, once you had been in her presence, you felt better for having known her:

> Being with her was always a blessing for me; I always came away a little bit richer—either my own thoughts grew clearer, or I came to see an old problem in a new light.[1]

Those who were fortunate enough to hear her speak were treated to a paradoxical portrait of a self-possessed woman of virtue and strength who exuded a deep humility, as described by one schoolteacher and audience member:

> I was expecting to hear an imposing, self-confident, female Jewish intellectual.... But instead...there appeared a small, delicate, surprisingly unpretentious woman...who clearly had no intention of impressing you by her demeanor and dazzling wit.... There was almost something childlike in the way she introduced herself....
>
> You immediately sensed a tremendous strength of intellect and an extremely rich, intensely disciplined interior life springing from absolute conviction.[2]

A fellow novice gives us a description of her that tells us more about her obedient heart and devotion to the Catholic faith:

> One of the things that struck me most about her was her devotion to prayer. The liturgy held her spellbound; at Mass she seemed to participate as if she were offering herself on the altar....
>
> She took correction with a humility that was genuinely edifying. It was clear that she wanted to use these occasions as a means of growing in holiness....
>
> There was something about her that inspired confidence and made you want to share her dedication. Even when it came to little things, she was always practicing obedience and trying to put aside her own wishes.[3]

Shortly after she professed her first vows on Easter Sunday 1935, Edith was visited by an old friend from her former life, Hedwig Conrad-Martius. She described the outward manifestations of the inner transformation of St. Teresa Benedicta of the Cross:

> Though Edith had always been friendly and childlike, the aura of childlike happiness and contentment she now possessed

was…absolutely charming. Grace and graciousness…had come together to form a unity.[4]

As I mentioned, I discovered Edith Stein at a very difficult time in my own spiritual journey. I, like Edith, had walked away from the religion of my youth in search of something greater or, perhaps, "truer." For almost twenty years, I stumbled through my life, falling out of grace and enduring the consequences of bad choices. I spent many of those years practicing New Age religions that were heavily steeped in the occult. To say that I was confused would be a dramatic understatement!

Remarkably, through it all, I never completely lost touch with the Catholic Church, and I even prayed to Jesus. However, the good things I remembered about being Catholic were overshadowed by the rebelliousness that I held in my heart over what I perceived to be a rigid Church hierarchy. At the time, I felt justified in my resentment toward an out-of-date, politicized, man-made religion that didn't value women enough to allow them a place at the table or equality with men.

If that sounds like a radical feminist agenda, it was; and it was fueled by a New Age frame of reference that places the human mind in the center of the spiritual universe and elevates human effort above all things. This type of worldview reduced God to an "energy source" at the beck and call of almost anyone willing to pay the fees to get trained to harness it. It all seems very ridiculous now, but understand that I was completely immersed in the error of my ways, even as I tried to play the role of "a good Christian" when it served me to do so. All of the wisdom, all of the gifts, all of the early burning flames of joy for the faith that were mine as a child as a result of having received the sacraments, were being squandered and were at risk of "dying on the vine."

The story of my return to the Church could be a book in itself, but let's just say that there was one Holy Spirit–driven moment of clarity that served to pick me up out of the New Age church and plop me back into the Catholic pews (last row, of course) with a force that could not be denied! Still confused and a little afraid, but humbled to the core, I began attending daily Mass during Lent of 1995. With each day that passed, my heart yearned for more. I had an almost unquenchable desire to learn about everything Catholic. I began attending Eucharistic Adoration (something I had never done before and didn't even know existed), learned how to pray the rosary, devoured the *Catechism,* and read my Bible every day.

My new sacramental life was deeper and richer than anything I had experienced outside the Church. The Truth cut like a sword through all the nonsense and confusion I held so dear prior to my return. I fell in love with the Catholic faith, and this time it was a love willing to grow in maturity that centered on my desire to be obedient to *all* of the teachings, which I discovered were not only profound, but completely perfect in their wisdom.

This transformation was initiated and continues to this day, almost two decades later, by the grace of God. I am nothing and can do nothing on my own. Everything I do in life—care for my family, work at my secular job, write about my faith, teach it, and share it eagerly with others through a speaking apostolate—is all done with a desire to love Jesus more and more.

In those early days of my return to the Church, that love was nurtured and nourished when the Lord sent me to a group of godly women who have been my mentors and sisters in Christ throughout the years. I have also been blessed by the example of good and faithful priests. And yes, I have been gifted with the spiritual friendship of a saint named

Edith who has shown me, and continues to show me, what it means to be a woman in the Body of Christ.

I "met" Edith Stein during those first years of my return to the Church through a collection of her writings for women published under the title *Woman* and translated by Freda Mary Oben, PH.D., in 1996. What first drew me to the book was the picture on the cover of a simple but intense woman. Her inner beauty sparkled through her dark eyes. She seemed "real" and accessible to me, even though she was Blessed Edith Stein at the time and destined to become a saint.

On the first page of the book, in the translator's preface, my eyes were drawn to one sentence: "In these essays, Stein teaches the woman how to be a balanced and fulfilled person in today's world."[5]

It was a bold claim, but one that was totally proven and confirmed by the time I reached the last page of the book. For me, reading Edith's words was akin to Dorothy opening the door of her farmhouse to reveal the Land of Oz! Suddenly, my spirit came alive in a kaleidoscope of new understandings and a clear vision for what it meant to be a Catholic woman. As I read each of Edith's essays, much of the confusion and hesitation I had about my role and place in the Church was replaced with a vibrant and heart-moving understanding that resonated deep within me.

I was enthralled by Edith's clarity and humbled by her example. Her straightforward teaching and lessons for women spoke to my heart, and I longed to embrace the truth that she herself had discovered and taught. If you have read the essays yourself, or studied them with a group, I am sure you understand those feelings. If you have not, I would highly recommend them. But for now, this book is my way of sharing the essence of her essays with you, to bring you along on the journey of my friendship with Edith. She continues to inspire and teach, and her voice still speaks the truth to us today. My hope is that she will speak to you through these pages and help you to understand who you are in Christ. Listen as she shares a beautiful and feminine wisdom for our souls.

HOW TO USE THIS BOOK

Chapter one will serve as an introduction to Edith's life. It will highlight the deep yearnings of her soul and offer you a glimpse into her heart. Chapter two will introduce you to her thoughts and begin to reflect on the influence that she can have on us today. Each chapter after that will correspond with a particular feminine attribute and explore insights and teachings that Edith/St. Teresa Benedicta wrote about or embraced in her own life. Much of her thinking and writing focused on the formation and true vocation of women and it is still relevant and valuable for us today.

In fact, many people acknowledge that Edith's lectures, writings, and lessons on the formation of women and the feminine soul seem to have greatly influenced the subsequent important and life-changing teachings of Pope John Paul II that have become known as the Theology of the Body. Professor John C. Wilhelmsson, in his book *The Transposition of Edith Stein*, explains: "John Paul II not only knew of Edith Stein but actually had a fairly strong connection with her."[6] This is because they were both friends with one Roman Ingarden, and all three of them were of the same philosophical mind, sharing a deep appreciation of phenomenology. Wilhelmsson reflects that "it is highly plausible that Wojtyla [Pope John Paul II], through his friendship and intellectual agreement with Ingarden, came to have a great deal of knowledge of and intellectual agreement with Edith Stein."[7]

Our former Holy Father, through 129 Wednesday audiences, has blessed us with a profound body of teachings that offers us a way out of the assaults on the dignity of the human person and celebrates the deep mystery and gift of human sexuality in the context of the divine plan and the mystical body of Christ. These writings significantly mirror points that Edith was making in her speeches and writings, while expanding upon them in a deeply practical way. Together, Edith Stein and Pope John Paul II act as guides and offer us essential wisdom and instruction on how to navigate the turbulent waters of our times and equip us with knowledge to combat the threats imposed by our culture of compromise and counterfeits. Throughout this book, there will be references made to the Theology of the Body and its connection to the life and thought of Edith.

At the end of each chapter, there will be a section entitled "Points to Ponder." These thoughts will invite you to think more deeply about the subject matter and to enter into prayer and conversation with Edith and Our Lord. You may want to write about these points in your journal or share them with a friend, spiritual director, or your women's group.

chapter one

Edith Stein: A Woman in Search of Freedom and Truth

"My longing for truth was a single prayer."

Dear reader, it is my great joy and honor to introduce you to Edith Stein.

Those who knew her have called her engaging, joyful, childlike, brilliant, and kind. If I were to describe in a single sentence the Edith Stein I have come to know, I would say: "She was a seeker who was guided by grace and who ultimately surrendered to Love."

Her life unfolded as a beautiful quest for authentic freedom and truth. There was a longing and restlessness in her that could not be satisfied by the things of this world—though her search led her to great intellectual heights and to a measure of worldly fame. Still, she also plumbed emotional depths that included times of deep despair, loneliness, and the questioning and subsequent "rejection" of her religion and prayer life. In the end, she received the gifts of a transforming grace and a spiritual peace from her Beloved Lord that would nourish and protect her, even as she came face-to-face with the greatest evil and tragedy of our times when she walked willingly toward her death at Auschwitz.

THE EARLY YEARS

When I encountered Edith Stein, I knew immediately that she was a different kind of saint. Born in Breslau, Germany, in 1891, she lived in the same era as our parents, grandparents, and great-grandparents. Like us, she lived through the turn of a century and in a world of great tumult and tremendous change. We can view her likeness in the many photographs that depict the phases of her life and gaze at the images of her family members, friends, and all those who influenced her and had an impact on the decisions she made. Much of what we know about Edith was written by her own hand, and several of her biographers have met her or knew her personally. All of this makes a heart-to-heart encounter possible. She is someone we can learn from and who, in all her humanity, lived a life that can touch our own lives through recorded memories, firsthand accounts, and the words she left behind.

Who Edith became as a woman and a Carmelite nun could not have been possible without the firm foundations of her Jewish roots and the strong example of her beloved mother. Edith was the youngest of eleven children, the baby of the family, born to Frau Auguste and Siegfried Stein. Her father died before her second birthday, but she enjoyed the attention of doting siblings and a special closeness with her mother. Edith was born on the Day of Atonement, or Yom Kippur, and according to Edith, her mother "laid great stress on my being born on the Day of Atonement and I believe this contributed more than anything else to her youngest's being especially dear to her."[8]

Although of the middle class, her family was not without its hardships. Frau Stein endured the loss of four children early in her marriage and the untimely and sudden death of her husband when she was still responsible for the care of seven children. To support them, she assumed the daily management of the family lumber business, which was struggling financially. Frau Stein took on this responsibility against the advice of relatives, and during this period, there was a great deal of family tension. As a result, Edith saw her mother make daily sacrifices for the family, and Frau Stein's example and conviction would greatly shape and foreshadow the type of sacrifices that Edith herself would make in later years.

More than anything, Edith witnessed the trust and reliance her mother had on God to carry out her daily duties. According to Waltraud Herbstrith, one of her biographers, "Frau Stein bore everything in union with God. Intelligent and energetic herself, she passed on these essential character traits to her youngest daughter. She was the formative influence in Edith Stein's development, the primary source of strength and affection for the growing child."[9]

Edith also enjoyed a close bond with her youngest sibling, Erna; they were said to be inseparable while growing up. Likewise, Edith benefitted from the guidance and teaching of her eldest sister, Else, who was often in charge of her care. Surrounded by these wonderful feminine and maternal figures, it is no wonder that Edith flourished both interiorly and intellectually.

When we think about the childhoods of saints, we often imagine that they were serene and exemplary in every way. We expect that, as children, their saintly tendencies were evident, or at least foreshadowed, but that was not exactly the case with Edith. By all accounts, Edith was a lively and engaging child, outstandingly bright and sensitive. She was intellectually mature beyond her years, in part because of her early and lifelong love for reading and learning. She even begged her mother for early admission to the Victoria School at the age of six—a request that was granted—and she was an excellent student there. However, when Edith didn't get her way, she was known to pitch a fit such that she would need to be locked in her room! In this account of her childhood, Edith speaks candidly:

During my early years I was mercurially lively, always in motion, spilling over with pranks, impertinent and precocious and, at the same time, intractably stubborn and angry if anything went against my will. My eldest sister, whom I loved very much, tested her newly-acquired child-training methods on me in vain. Her last resort was to lock me in a dark room.... Screaming at the top of my lungs, I hammered on the door with both fists until my mother would finally declare we were exceeding the limit of tolerance to be expected of the other tenants; she then set me free.[10]

The innate sensitivity and high temperament of her youth, which eventually grew into a mature, selfless compassion and empathy in adulthood, caused Edith both confusion and pain as a child. Edith explained, "Whatever I saw or heard throughout my days was pondered.... The sight of a drunkard could haunt and plague me for days and nights on end."[11] By the age of seven, this keen awareness of the problems and plights of others caused Edith to become so interiorly focused that she described it as leading a strange double life, one in which she felt lonely and separated from others, including her beloved mother and family members. Carrying this inner burden often compromised her physical health. She relates:

I never mentioned a word to anyone of these things which caused me so much hidden suffering. It never occurred to me that one could speak about such matters. Only infrequently did I give my family any inkling of what was happening: for no apparent reason, I sometimes developed a fever and in delirium spoke of the things which were oppressing me inwardly.[12]

In spite of Edith's rich interior imagination, an emerging sense of self-possession and control allowed her to develop a distinct firmness of character that was coupled with a great desire for freedom and independence. She wanted to be taken seriously and was impatient with those who treated her as a child. As Edith explained, "In my dreams I always foresaw a brilliant future for myself. I dreamed about happiness and fame for I was convinced that I was destined for something great."[13] She was ever anxious to answer that call—and school afforded her the opportunity to pursue her destiny.

Edith consumed her studies as if each lesson were her last meal, nourishing her mind and intellect to complement her active interior life. Edith said of those early school years, "Gradually my inner world grew lighter and clearer."[14] As Edith learned and grew, her world opened up, and she began to look beyond the sphere of influence of her family and friends. This included a questioning of the religion of her birth that led her on a quest for truth. By the time she had reached the age of thirteen, Edith had made the decision to stop praying.

At about the same time, Edith decided that she was finished with school. "I believe…a healthy instinct was the decisive factor. It told me I had been sitting on a schoolbench long enough and needed a change."[15] Edith was clearly burned out and, by some biographers' accounts, depressed. I cannot help but think this decision was fueled by a deep restlessness within Edith that launched her on her quest for truth and meaning. I believe it also was the beginning of her formation as a future teacher, for what she found lacking in those who taught her, she was eager to embrace for those she would one day have in her own classrooms. In fact, it seems everything Edith went through in her life laid the foundation for the next phase of her journey.

Edith's mother supported her decision to leave school, mainly because it was obvious that the stress of it was having an impact on Edith both physically and emotionally. As a means to recover and regroup, Edith went to stay with her married sister, Else, in Hamburg. Intending to stay a matter of weeks, she remained instead for ten months. There she experienced a prolonged period of pondering, coupled with the routine practicalities of domestic life. While her spiritual life remained in limbo during this time, the emotionality of her youth swiftly blossomed into a vibrant womanhood that brought greater maturity and a balanced and cheerful reserve that would become the hallmark of her personality.

The structure and routine that brought balance into Edith's life led her many years later as a scholar and teacher to extol the value of solid hard work as the "natural remedy against all typical feminine defects."[16] Indeed, Edith returned home renewed and more confident. Even her physical appearance changed, as "the slim child blossomed to almost womanly fullness;…the blond hair of childhood darkened noticeably" such that she was mistaken for one of her cousins.[17]

Prior to going back to school in the eleventh grade, Edith required extensive tutoring in mathematics and Latin to make up for time lost and to get back on the level of her peers. According to her, this time of rigorous preparation was to be remembered:

> This half-year of intense work I have always remembered as the first completely happy time of my life. That may be attributable to the opportunity given me a first time here: to have my mental powers fully engaged in a task for which they were eminently suited. When I sat alone at the desk in the room given me for my work…I was totally oblivious of all the world outside.[18]

Can't you just imagine a young Edith, hunched over her books, filled with the exhilaration of learning and completely engaged in her quest for knowledge and truth? God most certainly gifted her with a brilliant and insatiable intellect that was to become the clear, yet narrow, path back to him, in a way that she could never have imagined.

A PHILOSOPHER IS BORN

Edith enrolled in the University of Breslau in March 1911 with a firm determination to become a teacher. Instead, her studies drew her into the new field of psychology, which she eventually found to be superficial and lacking. Then, after reading a life-changing work by Edmund Husserl, Edith discovered philosophy, in particular, phenomenology. After four semesters, she had outgrown the university and followed her newfound and all-consuming interest to where Master Husserl was training in Göttingen. She delighted in learning and was indeed a natural-born phenomenologist. To this day, she remains one of the foremost leaders in this philosophical school of thought, joining the ranks of other influential figures such as her mentor, Edmund Husserl, Martin Heidegger, Jean-Paul Sartre, and Dietrich von Hildebrand.

Throughout her time in Göttingen, Edith flourished intellectually and socially. While there, she was free to engage in deep philosophical conversations with her contemporaries while still enjoying all the social activities and cultural opportunities of the region. She was also active in political affairs, along with her friends, by championing the rights of women to vote, work, and participate integrally in all levels of society. Her roommate at the time, Rosa Bluhm-Guttman, said of Edith:

> She was the most gifted woman I have ever met in my life—and I have known many extraordinary women.
>
> Edith had a deep love for truth. She had a penetrating and creative mind that kept on working at a problem until the truth came to light.[19]

Edith immersed herself in academic life, stunning her professors with her extraordinary grasp of phenomenology, all the while continuing to experience a spiritual dryness, maybe even drought, and clinging to the questions that drove her heart onward in search of an absolute truth in which she could trust and believe.

She received some relief when she attended the lectures of Max Scheler, a fellow phenomenologist and devout Catholic. Of him she wrote: He "affected me...far beyond the sphere of philosophy.... He was quite full of Catholic ideas...and employed all the brilliance of his spirit and his eloquence to plead them."[20] Edith was deeply impressed, though not transformed by her encounters with Scheler, as they did not lead her directly to conversion. She explains, It was "my first encounter with this hitherto totally unknown world. It did not lead me as yet to the Faith. But it did open for me a region of 'phenomena' which I could then no longer bypass blindly."[21]

With each intellectual encounter, Edith's heart was also beginning to open, as she began to meet and observe others who seemed to emulate and put into practice the ideals of which Max Scheler spoke. Two such influential guides were her good friends Adolf Reinach and his wife, Anna, who were Lutheran converts. Even after her first meeting with them, Edith felt as though she had stumbled upon a whole new world, a world in which people remained good-hearted and full of faith, in spite of their circumstances.

There were other encounters with people who began to expand her mind and sense of spirituality, but one pivotal meeting stands out from the time when Edith was a doctoral student. It would prove to be a brief, but life-changing, exchange with a stranger that made an indelible impression. On a visit to Frankfurt, she and a friend entered the cathedral there. This is how Edith described it:

> While we looked around in respectful silence, a woman carrying a market basket came in and knelt down in one of the pews to pray briefly. This was something entirely new to me.... Here was

someone interrupting her everyday shopping errands to come into this church, although no other person was in it, as though she were here for some intimate conversation. I could never forget that.[22]

What strikes me the most about this encounter is that, as intelligent and knowledgeable as Edith was and as satisfied as she was with her ever-widening circle of friends, she never closed her mind or heart to new ideas and experiences. Her keen sense of observation and engagement with the world around her wasn't just an intellectual exercise, but ever a spiritual one, as well. Without really understanding it, she remained open to the invisible hand of grace that was surely guiding her. The memory of that praying woman stayed with Edith all her life and perhaps defined the way in which she came to know and love God: through a profoundly personal and prayerful relationship that sustained and fulfilled her to her dying day.

A NEW BEGINNING

At the outbreak of World War I, Edith followed her fellow students and professors, including Adolf Reinach, into service. She volunteered with the Red Cross, requesting to work at a military hospital for infectious diseases, tending to Austrian soldiers. She seemed to revel in the opportunity to fully offer her heart in service to others. As she wrote of that time:

> My life isn't my own anymore. All my energy belongs to the great undertaking. When the war is over, if I'm still alive, then there'll be plenty of time to think about my own affairs again.[23]

This time of service is reflective of Edith's sense of patriotism, which remained strong all of her life.

Clearly, her early vanity was giving way to the examples of selflessness and Christ-like traits that were winding their way into her consciousness. Through her experience in the Red Cross, Edith was developing a servant's heart and a sense of deep resonance with virtues that were so much a part of her growing circle of Christian friends. It was at this time that another profound experience would shape the course of Edith's life.

Up until that point, nothing had more of an impact upon her than the death of her beloved friend Adolf Reinach. He died on the battlefront in November of 1917. Edith was crushed in spirit and eager to assist her friend Anna, his widow. Upon paying her a visit, Edith expected to find a woman beside herself with grief. Instead, Edith was "struck by Anna's courage, her ability to stand tall in the midst of grief. Here was a woman who, in her own way, carried divine life as she carried the cross of Christ…. Through Anna, Edith was introduced to the living person of Christ."[24] This was the new beginning that Edith had been searching for her entire life:

> For the first time I saw before my very eyes the Church, born of Christ's redemptive suffering, victorious over the sting of death. It was the moment in which my unbelief was shattered. Judaism paled, and Christ radiated before me: Christ in the mystery of the cross.[25]

This experience was a significant signpost along the road to Edith's conversion, but two additional incidents contributed to her complete surrender to the life that the Lord had been preparing her for all along.

Even though Edith was a gifted scholar, she could not obtain a teaching position at the university level upon graduation because she was a woman and a Jew. This was a professional setback that created a personal crisis for her. She was also trying to make sense of the growing embers of a newfound faith that were burning deep within her. Her unspoken desire to become Catholic was so contrary to the expectations of her family, and especially her mother, that she kept it hidden, at great emotional and personal cost. She returned home, where she kept in her office a large picture of St. Francis of Assisi. It was the only outward sign she gave of what was an intense inner turmoil. Edith described, "At the time my health was very poor, probably as a result of the spiritual conflicts I then endured in complete secrecy and without any human support."[26]

The next and final guidepost on her journey toward truth came in the form of a book. While visiting her friend Hedwig Conrad-Martius in the summer of 1921, Edith stumbled upon a copy of the autobiography of St. Teresa of Avila. She read the entire book in one sitting, and when she finished declared, "This is the Truth!" In St. Teresa, Edith found a kindred spirit and an example of someone who lived for and loved Christ. Edith immediately obtained a copy of the *Catechism of the Catholic Church*, and through prayer and intense study, she came to know Christ. During those months immediately following her conversion experience, she described her "yearning for Christ as one continual prayer."[27] Edith was finally baptized a Catholic on January 1, 1922, receiving her first holy Communion the very next day.

THE LONG WAIT

As one might suspect, Edith's mother, Frau Stein, was not elated with this most recent decision by her youngest daughter. But Edith did not expect her mother's reaction—which was to weep uncontrollably—and was deeply distressed to be such a source of sorrow for her mother. She had expected Frau Stein instead to be angry, so the tears and sadness were a true cross for Edith. Therefore, out of respect for her mother and at the urging of her spiritual director, Edith put her heart on hold and did not enter the Carmelite order, as was her deep desire from the moment of her baptism.

In her early years as a Catholic, Edith "was of the opinion that to lead a religious life meant one had to give up all that was secular and to live totally immersed in thoughts of the Divine,"[28] but as she grew in her faith, she learned to accept that what gifts she had been given were meant to be used for the good of others and in service to the world. To that end, she remained obedient and took up teaching at the Dominican sisters' school in Speyer for the next eight years.

Edith valued and embraced her vocation of teaching and possessed an innate sense of her students' unique needs for formation. Her deepening Catholic faith permeated her profession and every encounter with her students, who included girls at the secondary school, teachers in training, and Dominican novices. One of them wrote about her:

> She really gave us everything...none of us has forgotten the magic of her personality. She provided an example simply by her bearing.... She was a still and silent person who led us only by what she *was*.... In her criticisms she was a perfect combination of kindness and fairness. We never saw her other than calm, gentle, and quiet.[29]

As a teacher, and later as a writer and lecturer, Edith demonstrated and articulated the importance of the intrinsic value of the whole human person. She said, "It is most important that the teachers truly have this [Christ's] spirit themselves and vividly exemplify it. At the same time they also need to know life as the children will find it.... We must make the effort to understand them; then perhaps we may yet be able to be of some help to them."[30]

During the years at Speyer, Edith led a prayerful and hidden life. She would often pray through the night and teach during the day, while also finding time to serve the poor. Those who knew her at the time were impressed and awed by how she was able to accomplish so much and still maintain a rich prayer life and connection with God. She explained it this way:

> I don't use any extraordinary means to extend my working time; I just do whatever I can. Apparently, what I can do increases in proportion to the number of things that have to be done. When nothing urgent is called for, my energy gives out much faster. Heaven evidently has a sense of economy.… It all depends on having a quiet little corner where you can talk with God on a daily basis as if nothing else existed…and regarding yourself completely as an instrument, so that you treat your most frequently demanded talents, not as something that you use, but as God working through you.[31]

These are beautifully instructive words for all of us. They reflect the growing trust that Edith had in her relationship with her savior, and what can happen when we, too, reach this level of trust in our lives. Many of us have a sense that we have much to do and possess deep desires to accomplish something great for the glory of the Lord. Sometimes, our daily lives and responsibilities even seem to get in the way of our spiritual aspirations. Edith provides us with the example of a humble "doer" who took on her everyday tasks in a deeply spiritual way with great effect.

Edith said later in life, "[God's] true followers will be progressively exalted over their natural limitations."[32] She experienced this as she surrendered in joy to the rhythms and routine of the Dominicans and thrived on the stimulating and creative work of teaching and forming others. In all of this, she was nourished and energized by the many, many hours she spent before the tabernacle, having developed a fervent devotion to her Eucharistic Lord. This, too, is our own font of spiritual motivation and good works.

For a total of eleven years, Edith waited to enter religious life and profess her vows as a Carmelite. Her obedience bore much fruit in those years. She rose to prominence as one of the premier leaders of the Catholic Women's Movement in Germany. She was invited to write, travel, and deliver talks on such topics as women's education and professions and women's role in the light of nature and grace. She wrote prolifically and was in great demand, as she poured herself out for others through her talks, provided counsel, and offered up prayer. Due to her heavy speaking schedule, she was eventually released from her teaching duties at Speyer. Her views, enlightened by the Holy Spirit and motivated by love, soon brought her back to the forefront of the secular world when in the beginning of 1932 she accepted a position at the German Institute for Scientific Pedagogy in Muenster. All the while, she nourished her spirit at the foot of the cross.

During her years at Muenster, Edith witnessed increasing racial hatred for her Jewish brethren. It no doubt anguished her soul, as she knew herself to be a daughter of the chosen people, as well as a chosen child of Christ. As a well-known Catholic scholar of Jewish decent, Edith was not safe in the face of the threat posed by the Third Reich, but she was not concerned for herself.

Consequently, she was moved to request a private audience with the pope, in hopes of urging him to write an encyclical on the dire situation confronting the Jewish people—her people. The request was denied. Edith wrote at the time of a conversation she had in prayer during Mass:

> I told our Lord that I knew it was His cross that was now being placed upon the Jewish people; that most of them did not

understand this, but that those who did would have to take it up willingly in the name of all. I would do that. At the end of the service, I was certain that I had been heard. But what this carrying of the cross was to consist in, that I did not yet know.[33]

These proved to be prophetic words.

On the Feast of the Good Shepherd, April 30, 1933, Edith entered St. Ludger Church with the intention to stay there until she had received a direct and undeniable response from God to her request to enter Carmel. Reminiscent of her childhood stubbornness, Edith was determined to stand her ground in this vow to discern her life's path! At some point during the thirteen hours of devotion, she was certain that she had received her answer. She immediately returned home and once more requested permission from her spiritual director, Archabbot Walzer. Due to the zeal of his directee and the mounting threat from the Nazis, Walzer relented. Within two weeks, Edith had finally received permission to pursue the path that was her heart's desire. After spending several months with her mother, who was by then quite elderly, Edith wrote, "surely my mother would prefer me to be in a convent in Germany rather than a school in South America."[34] The archabbot described an elated Edith as someone who "simply ran to Carmel like a child into its mother's arms.... Once the situation in the Third Reich made it impossible for me to deter her any longer... she simply...heard the voice of the All High, followed it, and did not ask for long where the road led."[35]

THE FINAL SURRENDER

When Edith arrived at the door of the cloistered convent in Cologne in 1933, she stood in front of it and reflected: "At last it opened, and in deep peace I crossed the threshold into the House of the Lord."[36] She was finally a Carmelite! It was then that Edith Stein, at forty-two years of age, became Sister Teresa Benedicta of the Cross.

On the significance of her chosen religious name, Edith wrote in a letter:

> I must tell you that I already brought my religious name with me into the house as a postulant. I received it exactly as I requested it. By the cross I understood the destiny of God's people.... I thought that those who recognized it as the cross of Christ had to take it upon themselves in the name of all.... Today, I know more of what it means to be wedded to the Lord in the sign of the cross. Of course, one can never comprehend it, for it is a mystery.[37]

We can hardly imagine what joy the fulfillment of the yearning for her vocation brought to her. Far from being daunting, the stark austerity of Carmel was welcomed by Edith. Observers commented that the rigorous life of the cloister actually made Edith look and act younger, as she embraced a new depth of childlikeness fueled by the holy environs she now called home.

For the nine years that she lived as cloistered nun, Sister Benedicta (as she was commonly called) remained generous with her time and talents and stayed connected with the outside world. Her sense of duty and charity filled her life and heart with prayer for others. The interior well of her soul was perpetually filled to overflowing through the hours she spent in front of the Blessed Sacrament. What bliss, what ecstasy it must have been for her to be united mind, body, and spirit with her beloved Lord!

Edith walked away from the relative fame of her scholarly contributions and intellectual achievements into the small, hidden cloister, where she willingly and lovingly became a spiritual child of God. She had longed for the poverty of life in Carmel. One particular example of this remarkable transition made an impact on me. Two of the most necessary and valued skills in Carmel were sewing and housework, and it is reported that Edith wasn't particularly adept at either one. In fact, it was said that she sewed very badly and that it was painful to watch her do housework because she was so clumsy at it. I am so glad to be in such good company! But Edith embraced these humiliations with great joy and good humor. A love like hers could not be contained, and in spite of her "limitations," she was loved by those who shared the cloistered life with her.

Edith grew in love through her daily prayer, sacrifices, and work. Her love could not be contained—and soon this holy woman would offer the ultimate surrender on her way to sainthood. For the outside world was growing ever more dangerous for the Jewish people, as the Nazi control of Germany took root, and the ugly threat had the potential to reach even inside the cloister in Carmel. In response, Edith and her biological sister Rosa, who followed Edith to the cloister as a Third Order Carmelite, were moved on New Year's Day 1939 to a safer location in Echt, Holland. Sr. Benedicta seemed to have a prophetic understanding that it would be a temporary shelter:

> I find my predominant feeling has been gratitude: for being allowed to live here…. That doesn't mean I'm not constantly aware that here we have no lasting dwelling-place. But as long as God's will is accomplished in me, I ask for nothing else.[38]

It is hard to write about the next and final phase of Edith's earthly life. It seems an almost impossible task to capture the essence of the tragedy and the triumph, to describe the deep paradoxical mystery and ecstasy of the cross of love that Edith was to carry in her final months and days. Edith wrote extensively while in Echt. Much of what she shared in letters and essays revealed the inner workings of her heart and the depth of her surrender. At the same time, she was asked by her Reverend Mother to research and write on St. John of the Cross, on the four-hundredth anniversary of his birth in 1942. Through that assignment, Edith became even more engaged in what she titled *The Science of the Cross.*

The book is a profound volume that is fitting as her last contribution of intellectual and spiritual writing. On the cover of the manuscript, Edith drew a tiny cross, encircled by seven flames: a simple depiction that belies the depth of meaning she gleaned from the works and life of St. John of the Cross. The fact that he became her final spiritual companion and guide in much the same way St. Teresa ignited her soul in faith in the beginning of her life in Christ is a perfect manifestation of Edith's interior spiritual reality. St. John illuminated her heart and confirmed her convictions, as can be seen in these prophetic words from Edith:

> If the soul wishes to share [Christ's] life, she must pass through the death on the cross with him: like him, she must crucify her own nature through a life of mortification and self-denial and surrender herself to be crucified in suffering and death as God may ordain or permit it. The more perfect this active and passive crucifixion may be, the more intimate will be the union with the Crucified and therefore, the richer the participation in the divine life.[39]

In May 1940, the Nazis invaded Holland, and by December 1941, all Jews living in Holland were required to report to the Gestapo to be registered, Sr. Benedicta among them. As we might expect, "she did not greet the officers with the mandatory 'Heil, Hitler.' She would not use her hands, consistently clasped in prayer or outstretched in self-surrender, to praise Hitler. Instead, this petite Carmelite nun looked at the Gestapo officer and said, "Praised be Jesus Christ!" She later remarked that it might not have been the most prudent action, but she had been struck by the reality of the 'battle between Christ and Lucifer.'"[40]

At five o'clock in the afternoon of August 2, 1942, as Sr. Benedicta was praying before the Blessed Sacrament, a knock came at the convent door at Echt. What the world would see as the hand of evil, Edith might instead have known in her heart to be the knocking of her precious Lord, calling for her to make her final act of sacrifice. Edith and her sister Rosa were arrested and given five minutes to collect themselves and leave the convent. From there, they were taken to one internment camp, then another. Imprisoned and not knowing what was next must have been terrifying, yet Edith had already embraced an authentic freedom that could not be taken away. Of it, she wrote:

> Holy obedience binds our feet so that they no longer go their own way, but God's way. Children of the world say they are free when they are not subject to another's will.... The children of God see freedom as something else. They want to be unhindered in following the spirit of God.[41]

There are many accounts of Edith's last days and hours. All of them portray a woman of calm repose and abiding peace. Great pains have been taken to accurately record the details and confirm the eyewitness accounts of what happened to Edith and her sister Rosa. What we know is they were taken immediately to a central camp at Amersfoort, where they arrived in the middle of the night. It was there that it became clear there was not going to be a reprieve for Edith or Rosa, for while Protestant Jews and others of Jewish descent were released, the Catholic Jews remained in custody. Despite the harrowing circumstances, witnesses described Edith as a figure of tranquility amid the sea of terror that surrounded her.

Peter Loeser, a survivor, witnessed Edith during these first hours of her captivity. He described her as "unworried or perhaps even cheerful.... This was so different from the attitude of the other prisoners, who seemed paralyzed with fear."[42]

The next steps on the journey were filled with intentional and deeply unjust indignities, as Edith and Rosa joined thousands of others who were transported to the central detention camp at Westerbork. This was "the beginning of the end," where people were processed like cattle. They endured hours of endless lines and bureaucratic busy work that was meaningless and physically and emotionally exhausting. Magnify a time-wasting stop by the border patrol or security at the airport today by a thousand and add the insulting, demeaning, and dehumanizing treatment that the prisoners endured, without food, drink, or amenities, and we might have a tiny inkling of what Edith and all of the others went through.

The mother of a Dominican priest who witnessed Edith during this time related a poignant portrait of our would-be saint:

> What distinguished Edith Stein from the rest of the sisters was her silence. Rather than seeming fearful, to me she appeared deeply oppressed.... She hardly ever spoke; but often she would look at her sister Rosa with a sorrow beyond words.... In my opinion, she was thinking about the suffering that lay ahead. Not her own suffering...but the suffering that was in store for the others.... Every time I think of her sitting in the barracks, the same picture comes to mind: a Pietà without the Christ.[43]

Another eyewitness, Julius Markan, gave his impression:

> Among the prisoners who were brought in on 5 August, Sr. Benedicta stood out on account of her great calmness and composure. The distress in the barracks, and the stir caused by

the new arrivals, was indescribable. Sr. Benedicta was just like an angel, going around among the women, comforting them, helping them and calming them. Many of the mothers were near to distraction; they had not bothered about their children the whole day long, but just sat brooding in dumb despair. Sr. Benedicta took care of the little children, washed them and combed them, looked after their feeding and their other needs.[44]

It strikes me that so many were able to give such detailed descriptions of the Jewish nun in their midst. I imagine that Edith truly stood out in her complete abandonment to the will of God in the midst of such evil. Her days spent at Westerbork were dedicated to service, as she waited with a small group of select others for whom a glimmer of hope was pending in the form of a temporary deferment. There was tremendous anxiety, uncertainty, and suspense, and just as it looked as if Edith was going to be granted a release, it was revoked. She would not return to the convent.

Following this final pronouncement, Edith, along with a small group of brothers and religious in the camp, had a meeting just hours later with messengers from Echt, which included two men she knew. Trying to ease the tension, they offered her a cigarette. At this, Edith laughed and remarked that she had done her fair share of smoking and dancing when she was a university student. Amazingly, but not surprisingly, members of that same group made this report of one of the last recorded encounters with Edith Stein:

When I offered her my sympathy, the brave Sister said: *"Whatever happens I am prepared for it. The dear Child Jesus is among us even here."* With a firm handclasp she wished God's blessing on me and mine. When I tried to express my own wishes she assured me we need not worry about them, because they were all in God's hands. When it came to bidding all the others good-bye, the words just stuck in my throat. The prisoners walked away in a group to their barracks, but kept turning to wave to us, all except Sr. Benedicta, who went resolutely on her way.[45]

Sometime, in the middle of the night of August 6, the prisoners at Westerbork were called up for deportation. Thousands of men, women and children boarded a train, bound for what we now know was their imminent death. And what has been undoubtedly confirmed is that among them was prisoner number 44074—Edith Stein. Records show that two days later, upon her arrival at the Auschwitz death camp on August 9, 1942, Edith, along with her sister Rosa and countless others, died in a gas chamber. Her surrender complete, Edith was finally free to greet her Beloved.

THEN AND NOW

It has taken me nearly a week to complete the writing of this first chapter, the longest time I have ever spent on a single chapter in my life. As I have written, I have experienced emotional highs and lows and shed some tears as well. It is the busy week between Christmas and New Year's, and I have struggled to share with you the entire life of someone so dear to me in a single snapshot of words on a few pages. In the midst of all of this, I must tell you of a tiny miracle that has transpired.

I was taking a break from writing and getting prepared to wrap some additional gifts for incoming guests. I had assembled in a pile before me all of the paper, bows, boxes, and bags required for the task. As I dug down deep into one of the bags full of bows, I heard a tiny clinking sound. Reaching down further, I pulled out a tiny framed picture of... guess who? Yes, it was an icon image of Edith Stein!

I had no idea how it got there and no immediate recollection of where it came from. As I rummaged through the rest of the bag, I noticed some other articles that I recognized as the possessions of one of my dear friends, Krista, who had passed away several years earlier. Suddenly I remembered the connection! I had given the tiny picture of Edith as a gift to my friend in celebration of our shared devotion to and friendship with Edith. When Krista died, her family allowed me to take back some articles to remember her by, including the tiny picture of Edith. I had forgotten I even had it.

Yet, I believe with all my heart that the perfect timing of this find was no coincidence, but proof that my two heavenly friends, Edith and Krista, were reminding me of their presence and coming to my aid with encouragement when I needed it most. Because of this, I am as certain as ever of the communion of saints and know that our friendship with them extends beyond the boundaries of our earthly lives to a spiritual kinship that endures. Krista loved Edith as much as I do and would always refer to her as "my Jewish friend." I had always thought that I would dedicate this book to Krista, but that godly incident sealed the deal. I guess I will have to wait to find out what exactly they were up to when they hid that unexpected surprise for me to find, just as I was writing this book about Edith to share with you.

I hope that you have already been drawn in by this woman of great faith and deep humanity. Edith Stein's life was well-lived, and her death has brought great merit and wisdom to the generations that have followed her. When Pope John Paul II canonized St. Teresa Benedicta of the Cross on October 11, 1998, he said that she is "offered to us today as a model to inspire us and a protectress to call upon."[46] The legacy of her devotion and desire for truth lives on in her words. The love that she had in her heart is alive and well. Come now, and let us learn from her wisdom as we explore the depth of her knowledge together.

POINTS TO PONDER

1. What aspect of Edith's personality intrigues you most? Why?

2. Which part of Edith's life experience do you relate to most?

3. Reflect upon this quote from Edith:

   Holy obedience binds our feet so that they no longer go their own way, but God's way. Children of the world say they are free when they are not subject to another's will.... The children of God see freedom as something else. They want to be unhindered in following the spirit of God.[47]

   How does it impress you? What are your thoughts?

4. If you could ask Edith one question, what would it be?

chapter two

Woman, Know Thyself

"Do not accept anything as the truth if it lacks love.
And do not accept anything as love which lacks truth."

When we think about the lives of the saints, we can easily get discouraged. We might think, "I could never be that holy" when we compare ourselves to the actions and accomplishments of those who seem super-saturated in virtue. Yet, saints are simply people who trust in God and take him at his word. They are people who have fallen in love with a savior who knows them completely—and they desire to love him back. This is something that is attainable, and even comes naturally, to our feminine hearts. The truth is that every one of us is called to be a saint.

I am convinced that women today are hungry for deeper meaning in their lives. We are struggling to understand who we are called and created to be. Most of us know the right things to do, and we follow the teachings of the Church so that we can do our best to live virtuous lives. Every day, I encounter women who are accomplishing extraordinary things to build up the Kingdom of God, whether they know it or not, just by living their ordinary lives in faith and trust. They come from all walks of life and love Christ and his Church.

Nevertheless, many of these women are also perpetually busy, endlessly exhausted, and secretly disenchanted with how their lives have unfolded. In moments of total honesty, they might admit that their spirits are lagging behind the activity in their lives. They might wonder when they will ever be able to catch up or catch a break. All of this action and reaction can lead to feelings, often hidden, of inner guilt that nag and whisper that they are somehow falling short or failing in their true vocation as women.

In fact, today's generation of women seems to be asking, "Can we really have it all? And if we can, do we really *want* it?" Even as the lives of women are more varied and creatively rich than at any other time in human history, our myriad of choices come with an equal number of distractions. The more responsibilities we have, the more potential stress we have. The more roles we play, the less likely we are to truly know ourselves. Even with the world as our oyster, so to speak, and with no limits to what we can become, women's sphere of influence still begins with our families and extends out into the world like so many concentric circles or ripples in a pond. And yes sometimes that pond feels like a virtual tidal wave when it comes to sorting through everything that needs to get done!

Some women have made the choice to stay at home against the tide of working women. Some are choosing to home school, embracing in a particularly concrete way their roles as the primary teachers of their children. Other women have the desire to carry this out but cannot due to economic responsibilities or other constraints on their families. Some women are raising and supporting children on their own. Others, though fulfilled by motherhood, see the value in also pursuing a profession that utilizes their gifts and talents outside the home. Still other women are not called to physical motherhood but instead take on the role of spiritual mother in the Church or in the community in which they live. And finally, we can't forget the women in our midst who are godmothers, grandmothers, and great-grandmothers; each one has a vital role to play.

Edith Stein has something to say to each of us, no matter what our station in life. While many of us may struggle with guilt and feel torn as we hop from one role to another, rest assured that Edith would be the last one to judge us. In fact, if we asked her, "Where do women belong today?" she would say, "Everywhere," for Edith believed that "the participation of women in the most diverse professional disciplines could be a blessing for the entire society."[48] She stressed that, as women, "we cannot evade the question as to what we are and what we should be."[49] Edith holds before us a vision and vocation of woman that *transcends* the roles we occupy or the duties that we carry out.

She challenges us to embrace and come to a deeper understanding of the essence of who we are as women and how we can make a unique contribution to the world and those around us. Edith believed that before we can carry out our specific roles and fulfill our God-given vocations, we need to "first become a person!... Before a woman can become wife and mother in a positive way, she must first mature in her own self-possession. Although woman longs to love and receive love, she must also become strong enough to be a true gift to another."[50]

It seems to me that this statement is a clarion call for our times: Woman, know thyself. One biographer of Edith said it another way: "Before they can be ready to assist others, women first need to be securely anchored in their own depths."[51] Because the very essence of our vocation as women is self-donation, the truth is clear that we cannot give away what we do not possess. What we need to possess is an inherent and soul-deep understanding of our dignity and worth as women in the eyes of God. We are not simply speaking of a psychological acceptance, but of a spiritual maturity that blossoms and bears fruit through the contemplation of our vocation as women as an outpouring of our intimate, loving relationship with Jesus Christ.

Edith suggests that this is only possible in the context of grace and through a life of interior prayer, reflection, and silence. From this place of inner tranquility and peace comes the self-possession that enables us to bring forth the power and strength of our witness in the world. For when we women truly embrace our God-given gifts and allow ourselves to be formed by grace, we become conduits of God's love. His tender and gentle mercy is expressed through us in a uniquely personal and life-giving way, as our genius as women bears good fruit in the world.

Now, I don't know how you feel about that, but for me, it is both inspiring and challenging at the same time. What does Edith really mean by this? How can we go about embracing these qualities and cultivating them in the hopes of sharing them with others? Edith has the answer:

> To have divine love as its inner form, a woman's life must be a Eucharistic life. Only in daily, confidential relationship with the Lord in the tabernacle can one forget self, be free of all one's own wishes and pretentions, and have a heart open to all the needs and wants of others.[52]

Simply stated, we will never become the women God intends us to be outside of the sacraments. The interior state of our souls determines the fruitfulness of all of our activities. The highest degree of divine love will flow through us to others when we are living sacramental lives. Think of the blessings that abound from the Eucharist: They are never-ending!

Why is the Eucharist so important? It has to do with the way God made us and our deepest longings as women. Edith clarifies this by stating that "the deepest longing of woman's heart is to give herself lovingly, to belong to another and to possess this other being completely."[53] Our desire for that kind of total surrender and self-abandon is uniquely feminine. It is a desire that also must be purified and given to God and not another person. How many of you know women who seek this type of intimacy and connection with others—whether it is a spouse, friend, or child—to their detriment? Maybe it's even something you struggle with yourself. All types of relationship problems result when women seek to fulfill all of these longings, in totality, through a human relationship alone.

However, a Eucharistic focus for our energies and desires will help us to channel these God-given longings so that we can be set free in our spirits and not be enslaved by the distortion of them. Edith puts it this way, "Only God can welcome a person's total surrender in such a way that one does not lose one's soul in the process but wins it."[54] As women, our desire for surrender can best be satisfied through a spiritual connection and relationship with God, through our Eucharistic Lord. He alone will complete us. We are so blessed as Catholic women to be able to avail ourselves of the grace that pours forth from this sacrament of love!

Edith warns us of some of the things that we need to guard against as a result of our feminine natures. They are superficiality, vanity, emotional distortion or imbalance, and the desire to control or overextend our boundaries when it comes to our relationships with others. Does any of this sound familiar? I know that I have struggled with all of these at one time or another in my life and probably will continue to do so in the future. We will talk more about these tendencies throughout the book and seek ways to overcome these exaggerations. Like a good teacher, Edith gives us the full story when it comes to these struggles that lead us away from the virtues we are called to express through our purified feminine souls.

Our Feminine Souls

While Edith acknowledges that "every human soul is unique, no one soul is the same as the other,"[55] she also draws "the picture of woman's soul as it would correspond to the eternal vocation of women" and terms its attributes as "*expansive, quiet, empty of self, warm, and clear.*"[56] These terms may seem a little bit hard to understand, so I will take the next few pages to clarify them, share some insights from reading Edith's writings on these characteristics, and relate them to our lives today. But first, here Edith explains further how we come to possess these qualities:

> It is not a matter of a multiplicity of attributes which we can tackle and acquire individually; it is rather a single, total condition of the soul.... We are not able to attain this condition by willing it, it must be effected through grace. What we can and must do is open ourselves to grace; that means to renounce our own will completely and to give it captive to the divine will, to lay our whole soul, ready for reception and formation, into God's hands.[57]

So it is clear that we cannot force, by any action of the will, these attributes that God will form by grace through our openness and surrender. They are already within us, waiting to be called forth. I liken this to God as an orchestral conductor who will coax out the beautiful melodies from each instrument to form a beautiful and pleasing composition. The music of our distinctly feminine souls emerges from our openness and the hand of grace that guides us toward spiritual maturity and the sublime femininity to which we are called.

Another way to think of these attributes is as facets of a diamond. They shine together to bring out the brilliance of the gemstone, which in this case is each feminine soul. Let's explore these attributes in hopes of coming to a better understanding of ourselves and our soul's eternal destiny.

An expansive soul is one that is open to all human beings and is inclusive and championing of all life as sacred, God-given, and of infinite worth. It is a soul that is primarily concerned with human relationships and the dignity of the human person. Women are uniquely equipped to care for, nurture, and continually cultivate life and life-giving connections and relationships among human beings. We are "wired" to foster these connections not just on a person-to-person level, but to build bridges within our families, at our workplaces, and in our communities. No matter what our sphere of influence, our expansive souls are particularly attuned to make right the wrongs of exclusivity, divisiveness, dehumanization, or destruction within relationships.

Given this, we can understand the important influence that women can have on our culture and in our societies. If each woman cultivated expansiveness within her soul, the fabric of our society would be knitted together much more tightly than it is today, and the strength of the bonds that women inherently nurture would bring back sanity and structure to our families and our world. Pope John Paul II said in his apostolic letter to women:

> The moral and spiritual strength of a woman is joined to her awareness that *God entrusts the human being to her in a special way*.... Our time in particular *awaits the manifestation* of that "genius" which belongs to women, and which can ensure sensitivity for human beings in every circumstance.[58]

Woman's awareness of her expansive soul needs to be heightened, because when it is compromised, misunderstood, or disregarded altogether, she can fall prey to what Edith refers to as an "unchecked need for communication."[59] This includes a tendency toward disingenuous curiosity and entanglement in relationships that are superficial and self-serving. Sadly, we live in a society that seems to promote interactions such as these that appeal to the fallen nature of women and are directly opposed to the virtues that women are gifted to cultivate.

When expansiveness in the feminine soul is degraded, it can lead us to become involved in and concerned about relationships only as a means for gossip or as a means to exert our own will upon others. Edith describes this as an *"excessive interest in others,* a perverse desire to penetrate into personal lives, a passion of wanting to confiscate people."[60]

That all sounds pretty harsh to me. Still, I have to be honest and admit that this is something I struggle with on a daily basis! And I have observed many women who intensely conjure up interest in idle chatter and gossip. In my own case, I find that it can take an almost supernatural self-discipline to resist engaging in damaging conversations with others. Even if the information is true, it can still fall into the category of sin known as detraction. All of this reflects the dark side of an expansive soul.

One of the ways I try to combat this, besides going to frequent confession, is to make a sign of the cross with holy water over my lips every time I bless myself as I am leaving church. It's a reminder to me of what we are told in the Scriptures, that the tongue is like a tiny little rudder that can steer a large ship quite far from the virtuous shores! (see James 3:4–5). Edith knows that this is one of women's premier weaknesses—something we need to take to prayer often, so that we can rise above it and allow our souls to expand as God intends.

I have been blessed by the example of several strong, mentoring women who, along with God's grace, have helped me to "extinguish the wildfire of the tongue." Before meeting these women, I had no idea how much damage I was doing with my mouth, yet they have not been afraid to gently but firmly offer counsel and correction when I have fallen short in this matter. We need more women of such courage who are willing to apply some influential virtue. As Edith said, "For women to be shaped in accordance with their authentic nature and destiny, they must be educated by authentic women."[61]

On the other hand, using our voices to edify, exhort, and encourage others can be the *positive* outpouring of an expansive soul. As women, let's make a pact to help each other rise to this ideal in all our relationships and teach each other as Edith suggested when she said that "teaching girls to know and understand the world and people, and learn how to associate with them, should be the essential duty of the school…. A right relation to our fellow creatures is only possible within the framework of a right relation with our Creator."[62]

SOULS AT RISK

Another critical example of how women can stray from embracing the spirit of expansiveness is when we disengage from our primary vocation to nurture all life. On a grand scale, instead of championing life, women are destroying it. This is very tragic, not just for women and their never-to-be-born children, but for our society as a whole. *Every feminine soul that is not embracing and protecting human life is in some way dying to its true purpose, highest calling, and greatest fulfillment.* For thousands of women, the grave consequence has been unspeakable soul damage, buried but festering emotional pain, and a fundamental alienation from the core of their being (where God resides).

The so-called pro-choice movement embodies the example Edith gives of women's tendency to "confiscate people" and the aberration that leads women to attempt to exert their own will upon others as a form of vanity. Instead of answering the positive and holy call to expansiveness, the mantra of the movement—"my body, my choice"— leads us to a counterfeit surrender into carnality that directly imposes a spiritual enslavement, whether we are aware of it or not.

This degradation of the attribute of expansiveness of the feminine soul has come at a great cost for women, who, with society, are suffering severely for a lack of knowledge of what genuine choice and freedom really mean. When we women truly understand the beauty and intention of our expansive souls and submit them to the Lord, abortion in our society will become unthinkable. Women hold the key to this potential victory.

QUIET, MY SOUL!

Hopefully you have been reading this book in solitude, tucked away in some quiet little corner of your life, but that's not likely! There is absolutely no doubt that we live in a boisterous and demanding world that is neither quiet nor serene. Yet quiescence is the natural state our souls seek.

A woman's soul needs to be quiet not just for herself, but for those who seek refuge in her. Women are charged to offer care and compassion to the least among us—the smallest, weakest, and most vulnerable in our midst. Edith speaks tenderly of those women "who have ears for the softest and most imperceptible little voices."[63] Ladies, the state of inner quiet and peacefulness that we seek is possible as long as we make room for "breathing spaces," as Edith puts it, and take time to rest in God. Edith reminds us that God is there in these moments,

> and can give us in a single moment what we need.
>
> Thus the remainder of the day will continue, perhaps in great fatigue and laboriousness, but in peace. And when night comes, and retrospect shows that everything was patchwork and much

which one had planned left undone, when so many things rouse shame and regret, then take all as it is, lay it in God's hands, and offer it up to Him. In this way we will be able to rest in Him, Actually to rest, and to begin the new day like a new life.[64]

Nevertheless, Edith was very realistic and understood the pressures that women are under. Here she gives us a snapshot of a "soul in agitation" to which virtually every woman I know can relate:

The duties and cares of the day ahead crowd about us when we awake in the morning (if they have not already dispelled our night's rest). Now arises the uneasy question: How can all this be accommodated in one day? When will I do this, when that? Thus agitated, we would like to run around and rush forth. We must then take the reins in hand and say, "Take it easy! Not any of this may touch me now. My first morning's hour belongs to the Lord. I will tackle the day's work which he charges me with, and he will give me the power to accomplish it.[65]

She observed that "many of the best women are almost overwhelmed by the double burden of family duties and professional life—or often simply of only gainful employment. Always on the go, they are harassed, nervous, and irritable. Where are they to get the needed inner peace and cheerfulness in order to offer stability, support, and guidance to others?"[66]

She not only asks the question but provides the answer, instructing that each woman "must know, or get to know, where and how she can find peace. The best way...is...before the tabernacle." But when that isn't possible and when a quiet hour is not an option and when there is no place to retreat to, "she must for a moment seal off herself inwardly against all other things and take refuge in the Lord."[67]

In our times, this advisement becomes an admonition against all of the noise that surrounds us. We are tethered to technology and exposed to the 24/7 barrage of information and noise that comes from it. Our connection to ourselves and our souls is disrupted by the static of all these distractions, and truly our souls are starving for silence. If Edith were alive today, I believe she would take special pains to implore us, as women, to show our children a better way to seek silence by demonstration with our own lives and in imitation of the Blessed Mother. How can our souls magnify the Lord when we can't even hear his voice?

Once the soul has achieved a measure of quiescence, then there is the hope and potential for it to become empty of self, as Edith prescribes. She said that "becoming empty and still are closely connected."[68] If we are honest, much of the interior angst and turbulence in our souls stem from a preoccupation with self. Issues of competition and comparison, concerns for security and self-preservation, fears of abandonment and rejection all contribute to an inner chatter or dialogue dominated and driven by a motivation to answer the question "What about me?"

Edith points out that we can be empty and free from this self-preoccupation and that our souls can and will be satisfied *from within* only by the grace and presence of God. In a particular way, Edith speaks of woman's destiny as being that 'gracious spirit' [that] wants nothing else than to be divine light streaming out as a serving love."[69] In essence, we are most deeply fulfilled when we lose ourselves in service to others. We give ourselves away so that we can possess our true selves and give ourselves completely to God, and our feminine soul will be its own mistress. We empty ourselves by the grace of God so that we will be free to give freely—though the spiritual paradox is that we will never be truly empty because the soul replenishes itself in fulfilling its purpose.

This emptying of self is perhaps one of the most difficult spiritual milestones to achieve, but is unquestionably the most rewarding. It requires a holy detachment that flows from the font of grace and trust in the Lord. Edith described it beautifully when she wrote:

> There is a state of resting in God, of complete relaxation of all mental activity, in which you make no plans at all, reach no decision, much less take action, but rather leave everything that's future to the divine will, "consigning yourself entirely to fate...." As I surrender myself to this feeling, new life begins to fill me up, little by little, and impel me—without any voluntary exertion—toward new activation.[70]

WOMAN'S WARMTH

According to Edith, by nature there is a potential warmth and softness to the feminine soul that differs quite fundamentally from the masculine. If we think of the soul as a flame, the feminine soul was meant to be a gentle and balanced one. Neither easily extinguished nor a raging fire, the purified feminine soul will emit constant warmth that glows from an interior disposition with its foundation on Christ.

Edith likens this natural warmth of a woman's soul to the glow and holy fire of the Holy Spirit. She goes so far as to say that we can "find the Holy Spirit in all works of womanly love and compassion, inasmuch as it is the Holy Spirit, as Father of the poor, consoler and helper, who heals the wounded, warms the numb, refreshes the thirsty, and bestows all good gifts."[71]

Our souls can gain their warmth by worldly or divine fire, but we, of course, want them to be fed by the heavenly fire of divine love. This is only possible through God's grace. Edith says that "when the heavenly fire, the divine love, has consumed all impure matters, then it burns in the soul as a quiet flame, which not only warms but also illuminates; then all is bright, pure, and *clear*."[72]

What has happened to women's warmth? Is it being extinguished under the weight of masculine pursuits? Do we mistakenly equate warmth with weakness? Edith says a warm soul "consumes itself and fails when it may be most needed; or it is augmented by a flying spark to the fire which destroys when it should only gently warm."[73]

We are all influenced, whether we are aware of it or not, by a culture that exalts brazen, unabashed self-promotion in place of humble kindness and human warmth. I see this especially in young girls who consider themselves "emancipated" from the prescribed roles of femininity that they perceive as outdated or limiting. They seem to have lost a measure of tenderness. What can we do to help these girls rediscover their innate warmth?

Perhaps we need to show them by example that a warm soul will radiate humility, tenderness, gentleness, and meekness—all of which are virtues and fruits of the Holy Spirit within us. Edith says, "In womanly purity and gentleness, we find mirrored the spirit which cleanses the defiled and makes pliant the unbending; it abounds not only in those who may already be pure and gentle but also in those who want to spread purity and gentleness about themselves." [74]

Many people who knew her commented on Edith's warmhearted nature and the gentle manner in which she interacted with others, especially her students. She embodied warmth that drew others to her, and she enjoyed many deep and enriching friendships as a result. A woman's warmth has the potential to be the healing balm for many of life's ills. How will we ensure that we, too, bring our unique and God-given warmth into the world?

BLESSED CLARITY

The last characteristic Edith ascribed to the feminine soul is the state of being clear. She reminds us that clarity at the soul level is not something we can achieve by our own efforts. Surrender to grace makes it possible. We are especially vulnerable to the confusions of our world today—a world that calls right things wrong and wrong things right. The shortest path to clarity and a clear soul is a holy detachment and obedience to God; however, our society is not at all interested in obedience. We are told that to be truly fulfilled and free, we must pursue all avenues of pleasure-seeking to satisfy our every whim and desire. We live in the land of "if onlys." If only I could have a better job, a nicer husband, a bigger house...then I would be complete. But, oh how confusing and complicated life becomes when we seek counterfeits!

I once knew a woman who was asked what her most sought-after possession in the world would be. Her answer: clarity. How wise! Though she was enduring great personal hardship and struggling mightily at the time, I was certain that she would soon possess what she longed for, as she was in pursuit of something very noble. In fact, if most of us were to think about it, we could probably all benefit from the desire for a clear soul. Edith said that "faith awakens a yearning for unveiled clarity."[75]

Another way to think about a clear soul is to consider its transparency. A soul does not inherently possess this quality, due to original sin. But it can be made transparent by the light of the Holy Spirit. A transparent soul is free of distorted self-images and a dullness that comes from slavery to sin and darkness. Edith relates a clear soul to the freedom of purity that is the fruit of obedience and contrasts this spiritual freedom with a worldly freedom:

> Children of the world say they are free when they are not subject to another's will, when no one stops them from satisfying their wishes and inclinations.... The children of God see freedom as [being]...unhindered in following the Spirit of God; and they

know that the greatest hindrances do not come from without, but lie within...ourselves.[76]

A clear soul embraces a singleness of heart and answers God's invitation to dedicate all of its faculties to him. When we answer this call, our lives become full and fruitful. To obtain a clear soul, we need to seek truth in the form of a person, and to embrace what Pope John Paul II refers to as "mastery of oneself."[77] Edith refers to it as woman's natural tendency towards obedience and service: "Obedient I feel my soul, always most beautifully free."[78] With a clear soul, a woman can become what she should be.

John Paul II echoes Edith's thoughts and illustrates the manner in which a woman's soul becomes expansive, quiet, empty of self, warm, and clear. The essence of her meaning and gift of self leads the soul to become a "mistress of itself." He goes back to the beginning and the creation of woman to illustrate this point and make the connection for us. Follow the words he shared in his General Audience entitled "Man and Woman: A Mutual Gift for Each Other":

> Genesis 2:23–25 enables us to deduce that woman, who in the mystery of creation "is given" to man by the Creator, is "received" thanks to original innocence. That is, she is accepted by man as a gift. At the same time, the acceptance of the woman by the man and the very way of accepting her, become, as it were, a first donation. *In giving herself... the woman "rediscovers herself"* at the same time....
>
> So she finds herself again in the very fact of giving herself "through a sincere gift of herself," (cf. *Gaudium et Spes* 24), when she is accepted in the way in which the Creator wished her to be, that is, "for her own sake," through her humanity and femininity. When the whole dignity of the gift is ensured in this acceptance, through the offer of what she is in the whole truth

of her humanity and in the whole reality of her body and sex, of her femininity, she reaches the inner depth of her person and full possession of herself.[79]

Are you beginning to see how we, as women, are mysteriously and wonderfully created to give and receive from God and give back our unique, feminine gifts to the world in return? It stands to reason that in order for us to give our gifts, we must first learn to receive. The next chapter will discuss this beautiful calling to receptivity that is ours as beloved daughters of God.

POINTS TO PONDER

1. Contemplate the following statement from Edith:

    Although woman longs to love and receive love, she must also become strong enough to be a true gift to another.[80]

    What does this statement mean to you? How are you a gift to others? What stands in your way of becoming strong enough to be a gift?

2. Review the characteristics of the feminine soul: expansive, quiet, empty of self, warm, and clear. Which characteristic do you relate to most? Which one the least? Pick one, and journal about how this characteristic is expressed within your soul and in your life.

3. In what ways are you being called to the "rediscovery" of yourself, as Pope John Paul II suggests in his writings? How will this rediscovery help you to know yourself and to become "anchored in your own depth"?

4. How would you describe your feminine soul?

chapter three

Receptivity: Opening Our Hearts

"The intrinsic value of woman consists essentially in
exceptional receptivity for God's work in the soul."

A couple of years ago, I was invited to speak before a small group of women
in my hometown. The topic was open-ended, so I took the subject to
prayer and asked the Lord what he wanted me to talk about. One word
kept coming to my mind and heart: receptivity. Now that's not a word I
use on a regular basis, but it was striking because, at that time in my life,
I was also seeking and praying for ways to keep an open heart. It was
probably no coincidence at all that the Holy Spirit led me on a path of
discovery to delve more deeply into this subject.

What I discovered was that receptivity is a great and wondrous
gift that is at the core of the call in our lives as women. Not only is
receptivity an attribute of our feminine genius, but it is a foundational
part of our nature and the functional form of our physical realities from
which all other feminine graces flow. John Paul II said, "A woman's
dignity is closely connected with the love which she receives by the very
reason of her femininity."[81] Women, we are created to receive!

I don't believe that we have even scratched the surface of the deep
mystery of this gift. Truthfully, we cannot fulfill our vocation to empty
ourselves in service and love until we have first allowed ourselves to

receive all that God wants to give us. Edith wrote a poem with opening
lines that beautifully illustrate this gift of receptivity:

> Who are you, kindly light, who fill me now,
> And brighten all the darkness of my heart?
> You guide me forward, like a mother's hand,
> And if you let me go,
> I could not take a single step alone.
> You are the space,
> Embracing all my being, hidden in it.
> Loosened from you, I fall in the abyss
> Of nothingness, from which you draw my life.
> Nearer to me than I myself am,
> And more within me than my inmost self,
> You are outside my grasp, beyond my reach,
> And what name can contain you?
> You, Holy Spirit, you eternal Love![82]

Don't those words remind you of something that Mary might have said
when she encountered her Spouse, the Holy Spirit, at the Incarnation?
The Blessed Mother is a perfect model of receptivity for us to follow.
Edith said that "the feminine sex is ennobled by virtue of the Savior's
being born of a human mother; *a woman was the gateway through which
God found entrance to humankind.*"[83] To ennoble means to "lend dignity
to" something or someone; God chose a woman to receive him, and
that is the most awe-inspiring gift and privilege imaginable! As beloved
daughters of God, we are invited to carry out the same kind of beautiful
and mysterious receptivity that our Blessed Mother did throughout her
life in cooperation with the Holy Spirit. And when we do, we will be
filled to overflowing.

When I was praying for a more open heart, I was doing so because I
realized that I had been erecting some interior walls. Too many activities

in my life were crowding God out of my heart, and I was putting up emotional barriers to the graces he wanted to give me. Added to that, I was mostly just praying in my head, skimming the surface of my relationship with the Lord, and not sharing any of the nitty-gritty, not-so-pretty aspects of my life at the time. When my prayers start taking on an overly polite and formal prayer-book tone, I always know that I am pulling away from God and not being receptive in my spirit!

A RECEIVING HEART

In *Mulieris Dignatatem*, Pope John Paul II explains that "Christ speaks to women about the things of God, and they understand them; there is a true resonance of mind and heart, a response of faith."[84] Isn't this a most beautiful, intimate portrait of women's special receptivity? He goes on to give the example from Scripture of this feminine responsiveness and receptiveness in the person of the Canaanite woman who begs healing for her daughter from Jesus, who in turn, seems to ignore her (Matthew 15:21–28). The woman persists, and Jesus is deeply moved by her openness. She receives the healing she asked for and, no doubt, a whole lot more.

This is a teaching moment for us. The Canaanite mother remained open in spite of apparent barriers and what looked to be a situation in which Jesus was not paying attention. She seemed to already have a heart knowledge that Jesus was trustworthy, so she pushed through any fear or doubt she may have had to reach him. Jesus was not being unkind in this scene from Scripture, but instead was inviting the woman to go deeper in her faith and her trust relationship with him. In doing so, he confirmed and reinforced her faith and brought great dignity to her and her situation.

Virtually every woman I know has been engaged at one time or another in fervent prayers for the well-being of her children, or even someone else's children, just like the Canaanite woman. Whenever a child is sick, at risk of harm, or has fallen away from God or the Church, you will find women on their knees, waiting to receive some sign or answer from Jesus. If you are in this situation as you are reading this, and it seems like God just isn't listening, I want to encourage you to keep on praying! Don't be discouraged if he doesn't answer right away or in the way that you think that he should. Just keep the dialogue of your heart open to him, offer him your gift of receptivity, and you *will* receive—much more than you asked for in the first place! Remember what Pope John Paul said: When Jesus speaks to women (and he always does), there is a resonance of heart and mind. Trust him.

Our faith is bolstered by our receptivity, and our receptivity is strengthened by our faith. Edith explains, "God wishes to let himself be found by those who seek him. Hence, he wishes first to be sought."[85] When women seek God with an open heart, full of vulnerability and trust, his presence is felt and brought into the world in a very profound and powerful way. And because our receptivity is such an important gift, we have to be especially mindful of the ways it can be compromised, or even blocked, in our daily lives. Edith has quite a bit to say about this.

Spiritual Receptivity

In the quote at the beginning of this chapter, Edith speaks of the natural and essential value of women resting in our *exceptional receptivity for God's work in the soul.* She explains that there is "an especially strong natural desire for...spiritually nurturing values...within the soul of woman. [We are] predisposed to love the beautiful, inspired by the morally exalted; but above all...[women are] open to the highest earthly values, the inexpressible ones which remain in the essence of the souls themselves."[86]

Isn't this one of the most validating things you have ever heard? We are "predisposed to love the beautiful." God surrounds us with an abundance of his beauty every day to take into our souls, via our five senses, just to give us a tiny taste of heaven on earth. When was the last time you noticed this beauty and stopped to drink it in to refresh your spirit? What are the high earthly values you cherish, promote, and champion? How have you been touched or transformed by the working presence of God in your soul in the last six months?

You might find these queries challenging or foreign to your way of thinking or relating to God. That's because today, women are at risk of being too busy, too tired, too stressed, and too distracted to open the gift and explore our unique receptivity as a means to appreciate the deep and abiding beauty that surrounds us. Yet God is calling us, every day. He wants to be found, and he wants to be received by women in the very depth of our souls. And where do we find God most profoundly? We find him in the Eucharist, of course. As Catholic women, we are so very blessed to be able to receive Jesus every day in this way. In fact, I believe that the more we receive our Lord in the Eucharist, the more capacity we have to appreciate and exemplify God's beauty here on earth. We also will be strengthened for all that we are destined to accomplish. As Edith explains:

> Through His sacraments, He purifies and strengthens us. And if we turn confidently to Him, which is His will, His spirit penetrates us more and more and converts us; through union with Him, we learn to dispense with human props and to gain the freedom and strength which we must have in order to be the support and mainstay for others.[87]

I love the phrase that Edith uses here—*we learn to dispense with human props*. That's what it's all about, isn't it? What are your human props?

Two of mine are worry and routines. I've discovered that in order for me to stay open and receptive, I have to let go of excessive worry because, for me, it becomes a vehicle (and an excuse) to take control over people, places, and things. The opposite of worry is surrender—the "red carpet" for receptivity. Surrender welcomes the divine flow of the life of the Holy Spirit, who makes possible the freedom and strength of which Edith speaks—and leads us to experience genuine bliss if we let him. Isn't that worth letting go of worry to receive?

I have learned that rigidity and clinging too tightly to my routines can also quash my receptivity. I have to pray often for a "flexible spirit" and to surrender my expectations to control a situation. I've discovered that I don't like interruptions—such as a traffic jam, an unexpected visit, or a decision by my husband to detour from my "to-do" list!—and can be a little rude when things don't go as planned. This is something that I *really* need to work on because sometimes the unplanned brings a beautiful surprise, and the interruption is its own reward. I need to be open to God's providence in all things and at all times.

Another way that we say yes to receptivity is to learn how to say no! Receiving with prudence means that we are to become good stewards of our energies and grow in wisdom on how we spend our time. It also means that we examine our emotional attachments and the nature of our commitments, considering them to be precious commodities that require a certain amount of personal detachment. As Edith explains, because "woman naturally seeks to embrace that which is *living, personal, and whole*,"[88] we sometimes bite off more than we can chew. Speaking of woman, she says:

> *Her view reaching toward the whole* leads easily to the frittering away of her powers: her antipathy for the necessary objective disciplining of individual abilities results in her superficial nibbling

in all areas. And in her relations to others, it is manifested in her complete absorption with them beyond the measure required.[89]

One of the things I love about Edith is that she never minces words! Her message is a warning that our receptivity can be unbalanced or lack discipline and discernment. Can we be too open? Yes. In the expression of our openness, we are still charged with exercising healthy boundaries that ensure we don't compromise our dignity and self-respect.

Yet there is still a greater attack on our receptivity that comes directly from the enemy of our souls.

PHYSICAL RECEPTIVITY
The devil is working overtime to twist and distort women's gift of receptivity, to the ultimate detriment of mankind as a whole. For we live in a culture that misuses receptivity by turning women into mere "receptacles." With this, the "hookup" mentality of our world tells woman that they are empowered when they are free to pursue multiple unencumbered sexual encounters, aided by the use of contraceptives. This is probably the greatest lie and mass deception the devil has ever been able to pull off.

Quite to the contrary, we need to be self-aware and champion our dignity by not allowing ourselves to become usable and disposable objects for the gratification of others. We need to safeguard the human tendency to dehumanize and exploit one another in a strictly utilitarian manner. When we trade the deepest desires of our hearts—to be cherished and give ourselves completely to another in a relationship based on mutual respect, love, and trust—for fleeting, superficial connections that are immoral and empty of value, we do so at the peril of our very souls.

Outside of the Eucharist, our fertility is the most profound mystery we can experience this side of heaven. Our bodies work in a symphony of hidden miracles that enable us, through the gift of receptivity, to become co-creators and life-bearers, both physically and spiritually. A deep and wounding schism and confusion results when we take actions to separate our bodies from our souls; when we place barriers between our natural physical reality and the spiritual essence of who we are and who we are called to be. Edith explains why this is so when she says:

> The relationship of soul and body is not completely similar in man and woman; with woman, the soul's union with the body is naturally more intimately emphasized…. Woman's soul is present and lives more intensely in all parts of the body, and it is inwardly affected by that which happens to the body.[90]

With this explanation and understanding, it is easy to see why the Church, in her infinite wisdom, seeks so vigorously to safeguard woman's gift of physical receptivity and fecundity. The very nature of a woman's soul is directly affected when her physical receptivity is thwarted.

When I first read the above words from Edith, I had the first of many "aha" moments on my journey back to the Catholic Church. Admittedly, I was never really a fan of contraception, for I felt that it was physically unhealthy and unnatural, and I feared the artificial manipulation of my body with chemicals whose names I couldn't pronounce. However, I did not abstain from contraception on moral grounds, but simply from not wanting to use foreign objects and substances to stop my body from doing what it was designed to do naturally. I called myself a "naturalist," and that seemed to satisfy the perplexed and furrowed looks of men and women who didn't quite get where I was coming from.

But after reading Edith's *Essays on Woman*, I was deeply affected by the reality that the use of contraceptives not only damages women physically, but spiritually, as well. I came to see it as the "falsification of the inner truth of conjugal love,"[91] as stated in the *Catechism of the Catholic Church*—that woman's inner truth is trampled upon and disregarded directly and most profoundly through the use of contraceptives.

Hungry for more on the subject, I was next stunned when I stumbled upon a website for the Edith Stein Foundation (www. theedithsteinfoundation.com)—a foundation dedicated to advocating the dignity of women through fostering a non-contraceptive culture! Here is the vision of the foundation:

> The Edith Stein Foundation seeks to expose the profound and tragic effects that contraception has had on women and therefore society as a whole. We desire to heal the individual and collective wounds through our educational efforts, and inspire a new generation of women to know, love and live the gorgeous dignity that is womanhood in the spirit of Edith Stein, German philosopher, feminist, and canonized Saint. We hope for nothing less than the renewal of culture through woman, family, and society.[92]

I do believe that Edith would be very pleased! The website also says of Edith:

> She would also see contraception and sterilization as a deeply traumatizing form of rejection of woman's core self. She would see them as debilitating compromises with fear and therefore contrary to reproductive freedom. She would not view contraception and sterilization as liberating technologies, but rather cruel instruments of woman's personal degradation and enslavement to the will and desires of others.[93]

Powerfully stated, this is most definitely reflective of what Edith said and stood for during her life. There is no doubt that Edith would support the foundation that bears her name and puts forward the latest in research and reason on the topic of the ill and lasting effects of contraception on women's minds, bodies, and souls.

Why is it essential for women today to understand the preciousness of our fertility? Because we cannot fulfill our true vocation and deepest longings when we place artificial barriers upon them. Contraception is not a "necessary evil" for modern society, as many contend. The Church does not restrict the use of contraceptives on the grounds of some archaic code of ethics to make our lives more difficult. On the contrary, the Church in her wisdom confirms the deepest truths of our being and supports actions that will lead directly to our greatest spiritual freedom by attempting to preserve and promote the natural gift of our God-given receptivity.

Innovations in natural family planning methods now make it possible for married couples to plan for their families in cooperation with God's grace and plan, in efficient and effective ways. The *Catechism of the Catholic Church* states that "these methods respect the bodies of the spouses, encourage tenderness between them and favor the education of an authentic freedom" (2370). In line with the natural, God-designed plan for procreation, natural family planning respects and elevates woman's receptivity as God intends, promotes greater physical health, and contributes to holier marriages.

There can be no greater declaration of feminine receptivity than when Mary proclaimed, "Let it be me according to your word" (Luke 1:38). Pope John Paul II, in his General Audience of December 6, 1995, pointed out that all women are called to emulate and carry out the sentiment of these words to benefit Church and society. Women are uniquely called to receive Christ and bring him into the world, as Mary did. As the pope explains:

The importance of woman's co-operation in the coming of Christ is emphasized by the initiative of God, who, through the angel, communicates his plan of salvation to the Virgin of Nazareth so that she can consciously and freely co-operate by giving her own generous consent.

Here the loftiest model of woman's collaboration in the Redemption of man—every man—is fulfilled; this model represents the…reference point for every affirmation of woman's role and function in history.

In carrying out this sublime form of cooperation, Mary also shows the style in which woman must concretely express her mission.[94]

GOD'S WORK IN OUR SOULS

Women are mysteriously and wonderfully made to receive God and all of his goodness and grace in a uniquely feminine and intimate way. To make this point, Pope John Paul II refers to an encounter between Jesus and another woman—Jesus's friend Martha, after the death of her brother Lazarus. The conversation, initiated by Martha,

> concerns the most profound truths of revelation and faith: "Lord, if you had been here my brother would not have died." "Your brother will rise again." "I know that he will rise again in the resurrection at the last day." Jesus said to her: "I am the resurrection and the life; he who believes in me, though he die, yet shall live, and whoever lives and believes in me shall never die. Do you believe this?" "Yes, Lord; I believe that you are the Christ, the Son of God, he who is coming into the world" (Jn 11:21–27).… *This conversation with Martha is one of the most important in the Gospel.*[95]

I think John Paul II emphasizes this last point because in this real and raw exchange, Martha represents every woman who has ever implored

Christ and remained completely open for his loving response to console and transform her by his teaching and his grace.

Edith states that "knowledge and love of God is won only by a continuous intimate communion with Him.... *That* woman who, everywhere she goes, brings along with her the Savior and enkindles love for Him will fulfill her *feminine* vocation in its purest form. Basically, therefore, woman's *intrinsic value* lies in making room within herself for God's being and works."[96]

I want to be *that* woman...don't you?

POINTS TO PONDER

1. How do you "love the beautiful" in your life? How are you inspired by what is "morally exalted"? What are the "earthly values" that make your soul swell with gratitude, praise, and thanksgiving?

2. Reflect upon the following words from Edith concerning a woman's soul.

   Woman's soul is present and lives more intensively in all parts of the body, and it is inwardly affected by that which happens to the body.[97]

   Do you agree or disagree? Why? How does this statement impact your understanding of the Church's teaching on contraceptive use?

3. What are the "human props" that get in the way of receptivity in your life?

4. How do you make room within yourself for God's being and works?

chapter four

Generosity: Freedom through Surrender

"The deepest longing of a woman's heart
is to give herself lovingly."

I could have entitled this chapter "Handmaids and Helpmates" because they are the most prominent women's roles exhibited throughout Scripture—culminating in their most perfect expression by our Blessed Mother. Yet, how do we relate to these roles today? What does it mean to be a handmaid, and how are we especially equipped to be a helpmate to others, especially to our husbands and the men in our lives? How do these roles reconcile with the realities of our lives as busy, active, faithful women in the modern world? The answers to these questions and more come straight from Edith's teachings on the formation of woman and her study of the spirituality of Christian women.

Most obvious is the fact that woman's generosity flows directly from her receptivity, for we cannot give what we have not received. And the nature and extent to which we are free to give of ourselves and our gifts are dependent upon the *depth* of our understanding of our true natures and the *breadth* of our trust and surrender to God's graces, as we embrace our roles as helpmates and handmaids. Let's examine this depth and breadth of feminine generosity through the mind and heart of Edith.

BACK TO THE BEGINNING

In order to truly understand and embrace the gift of generosity, we need to go back to the beginning of Genesis and reflect upon what it says:

> So God created humankind in his image...male and female he created them. (Genesis 1:27).

Also:

> But for the man there was not found a helper fit for him. So the LORD God caused a deep sleep to fall upon the man, and while he slept took one of his ribs and closed up its place with flesh; and the rib the LORD God had taken from the man he made into a woman and brought her to the man. (Genesis 2:20–22)

In our world today, women's roles have become confused and distorted, and our souls have been damaged in the process. We have forgotten our true nature and calling to be generous helpmates to others. God created us for this purpose, and we have not fundamentally changed or evolved from this original vocation. We draw greater meaning and deeper clarity from our lives when we embrace this destiny because, as Edith says, "Woman's destiny stems from eternity. She must be mindful of eternity to define her vocation in this world. If she complies with her vocation, she achieves her destiny in eternal life."[98]

Edith explains the role of helpmate most beautifully, in a way that most women—whether married or single, in the working world or working within the home—can relate to:

> The woman who "suits" man as helpmate...complements him, counteracting the dangers of his specifically masculine nature. It is her business to ensure to the best of her ability that he is not totally absorbed in his professional work, that he does not permit

his humanity to become stunted, and that he does not neglect his family duties as father. She will be better able to do so the more she herself is mature as a personality; *and it is vital here that she does not lose herself in association with her husband but, on the contrary, cultivates her own gifts and powers.*[99]

When I first read these words by Edith, I was so excited! I had never heard woman's role of helpmate described in such an affirming and uplifting way. Edith's words were in direct contrast to the feminist rhetoric that had shaped my relationships up to that point. That rhetoric proclaimed that in order to be happy and satisfied, I had to strive to have it all—everything that a man had and more—and be fiercely independent and autonomous, at all costs. I was tricked into believing that if I settled for anything less, I would be at risk of losing myself and my whole identity to the demands and whims of the male-dominated world. Especially within the marriage relationship, the feminist agenda was to achieve equality and power, at the expense of a generous service for the benefit of the other!

I now understand how contaminating and contradictory that message was to my very soul. It is an exploitation and exacerbation of all that can go wrong in a marriage due to the Fall. When Adam and Eve first walked the earth, they did so in perfect harmony with one another in what Edith referred to as "the most intimate community of love" and what Pope John Paul II calls "the unity of the two." According to Edith, before our first parents sinned, "all faculties in each individual were in perfect harmony, senses and spirit in right relationship with no possibility of conflict. For this reason, they were also incapable of inordinate desire for one another."[100] In essence, woman as helpmate was an integral extension of her nature and could not be separated from her identity.

However, as a consequence of original sin, man and woman see "each other with different eyes" and have "lost innocence of interchange with one another."[101] Instead of harmony, there is the potential for division; instead of unity, there is the potential for competition; and instead of a natural, flowing generosity, there is the potential for a destructive selfishness. We need to guard against any so-called advice or cultural context that fuels the flames of these tendencies that can be so damaging in our relationships with each other.

Instead, Edith urges us to go deeper in our explorations of the true nature of our souls and examine the truth that is written on our hearts about who we are and who we are created to be. What Edith describes here is a supernatural generosity of spirit that, when cultivated by women who pray for and possess it, can have significant impact on others in their families and beyond. This generosity of spirit goes deeper than the giving of tangible and material things. It reflects an interior freedom that does not count the cost; that expends lavish good will upon others, especially one's spouse, which includes seeing the best in him, desiring his highest good, and giving of oneself in pursuit of that end.

Edith encourages us to cultivate this truth and put into action the gifts we have been given to become true helpmates for the benefit of everyone with whom we come into contact. In this way, we will become fulfilled and successful women, not *in spite* of our femininity but *because* of it!

THE FEMININE VOCATION

Edith lived at a time when a woman's sphere of influence was still predominantly within the home, where she occupied the roles of wife and mother. While Edith stressed these roles as being the most important and God-ordained, she also championed the idea that "there is no profession which cannot be practised by a woman…. A self-sacrificing woman can accomplish astounding achievements when it is a question of replacing the breadwinner of fatherless children, of supporting abandoned children or aged parents." A woman's individual gifts and talents give "her the capability of doing professional work, be it artistic, scientific, technical, etc."[102] With these ideas, Edith presented a forward-thinking feminism that took into account the spiritual nature of women and the need for an adequate educational formation in the process.

Today, we take it for granted that women can do just about any type of work and pursue any profession to which they feel called. But what we might not fully understand is the way in which we are *especially equipped to bring our unique feminine gifts to bear* in the workplace and the sphere of our professional lives. Generosity, in particular, is a spiritual attitude and attribute that is needed in the marketplace and one that women possess in a special way in order to bring balance, compassion, and empathy to the dog-eat-dog world of work.

Edith explains that in certain fields, especially when a woman develops her feminine nature at work, it can "become a blessed counterbalance…where everyone is in danger of becoming mechanized and losing his humanity."[103] This was a radical concept for Edith's time, and she pushed the envelope herself by remaining a single working woman in the upper echelons of academia where the most prominent positions were occupied by men. Yet, with all her prominence and influence, Edith encountered her own glass ceiling when she did not achieve full professorship at the university level because she was a woman. Still, she insisted that "the participation of women in the most diverse professional disciplines could be a blessing for the entire society."[104]

In our modern world, we must constantly battle against greed and the commodification of human beings. Making a profit at all costs has infiltrated nearly every aspect of our society and every profession, including the human services and so-called nonprofit sectors. I can relate to this as an administrator for a nonprofit organization where I spend my days trying to balance the needs of people, despite a shrinking bottom line and a limited reserve of resources. Sometimes we have to make tough choices and strive to do the least amount of harm. In this environment of materialism, everything is subject to a cost-benefit analysis, and we are often pressured to overlook or undermine the truth that every human life is of priceless value.

As I have grown to understand the feminine genius, as it is described by Edith and Pope John Paul II, I have experienced the fruitfulness that can come when, in the face of worldly stressors, I remember that I am uniquely equipped to relate generously to others, not just within my family, but with those I contact through my job. For a long time, I fought the idea that I had to go outside the home to work for economic and practical reasons. As a newly reverted Catholic mom, I envisioned a life where I could stay at home, teach, and raise my child in the secure bosom of our little domestic church. Unfortunately, life and my husband had a different vision!

After the first five years of my daughter's life, a compromise was struck, with a little help from my spiritual director, and I surrendered to the need for me to go outside our home to work. Even as I committed my work life to the Lord, I found it extremely challenging because I never felt as though I was doing justice to either of my worlds. That whole agonizing process reminds me of how Edith must have felt when, after she finally discovered the truth in Catholicism, she could not enter religious life.

Even as Edith's heart and mind were telling her to follow her calling to give herself completely to the Lord at Carmel, the practicalities and her life circumstances called for something altogether different. In a letter to a religious friend, she relates how ultimately God's will led her to remain firmly planted in the secular world, at least for a time:

> Immediately before, and for a good while after my conversion, I was of the opinion that to lead a religious life meant one had to give up all that was secular and to live totally immersed in thoughts of the Divine. But gradually, I realized that something else is asked of us in this world and that, even in the contemplative life, one may not sever the connection with the world. I even believe that the deeper one is drawn into God the more one must "go out of oneself"...to the world in order to carry the divine life into it.[105]

But we know that God used that time in Edith's life to bear much good fruit. And he has blessed me, as well. He can do the same in all of our lives when we humbly and obediently submit to his will, even when it goes against the desires of our heart.

In my case, God's will was different from mine, but rather shortly after my own personal surrender, he showed me in many powerful ways how I could bring the feminine call of generosity into my relationships with coworkers and everyone else I encountered throughout the workday. Over time and with a fair amount of grace, I have been able to shift my focus from trying to get ahead and being the best at work to helping others and serving them with empathy and compassion so they can reach *their* highest potential. As my understanding of the concept of servant leadership, combined with the feminine gifts God has given me, has unfolded in my work life, I have experienced a deep satisfaction on the job that I previously could never have imagined. I now look upon work much more as a vocation than as a job or career, and I am able to trace the workings and handiwork of the Holy Spirit in my professional interactions.

Edith provides us with a perfect model for how we can bring generosity into the workplace for the benefit of all. She points to the Blessed Mother at the wedding at Cana:

> In her quiet and observing looks [she] surveys everything and discovers what is lacking. Before anything is noticed, even before embarrassment sets in, she has procured already the remedy. She finds ways and means, she gives necessary directives, doing all quietly. She draws no attention to herself.[106]

Edith says:

> Let her be the prototype of woman in professional life…. Let her always perform her work quietly and dutifully, without claiming attention and appreciation. And at the same time, she should survey the conditions with a vigilant eye. Let her be conscious of where there is a want and where help is needed, intervening and regulating as far as it is possible in her power in a discreet way. Then will she like a good spirit spread blessing everywhere."[107]

Two Women

Our call to generosity is so empowering! I believe that it is the key to success in any occupation or endeavor. But there are many ways in which the gift of generosity can be blocked within us. We can see the outward signs of this in others and in ourselves when we fall prey to narcissism, self-centeredness, a guarded spirit, or materialism. These actions and attitudes reveal the deeper wounds that drive us to grasp for fulfillment, affirmation, and comfort in all the wrong places and leave us unable or unwilling to give anything of ourselves to others in a loving and selfless way. You may know someone like this or maybe you have battled against these distortions in your own life. Jesus encountered such a woman at the well.

In Scripture, we hear her story (John 4:7–29). The woman at the well is a Samaritan woman who Jesus meets at midday. They engage in the longest conversation Jesus has with anyone in the Bible, in which he reveals the deepest mysteries of God. Yet, when Jesus first approaches her, she is cautious and suspicious. Through the course of their conversation, the woman reveals a long history of broken relationships in her quest for authentic intimacy. As she opens her heart to Jesus, she recognizes that she has come face-to-face with someone who knows everything about her and still accepts her. This encounter has a profound effect upon her; it unfreezes her heart and opens her soul to flow with a generous and genuine love.

In some ways, each of us is that woman at the well. We have our walls and secrets, our heartaches and masks. Yet just as Jesus speaks to the Samaritan woman of living water, he speaks to us and tells us that he is the source of life and a wellspring of love, virtue, and grace that will never run dry. It is from him that the gift of generosity flows. I find the story of the woman at the well to be one of the most beautiful in the Bible, for it portrays the potential for such an intimate encounter with Jesus, a possibility for all of us who are willing to allow him to meet us in the midday of our own brokenness.

Contrast the woman at the well with the account of the woman at Bethany (Matthew 26:6–13). In this story, a woman enters the house of Simon the leper uninvited and sits at the feet of Jesus, anointing them with expensive perfume. She lavishly pours the liquid, which would have been worth close to ten thousand dollars today. Beyond the monetary expense were the sentiments of complete devotion and unrestrained love and gratitude that were behind her humble gesture.

The biblical account makes reference to the fact that she broke open the bottle as another way of expressing her wholeheartedness. She did not count the cost. Her act was extravagant in every way and completely impractical. But it was also reflective of the inner freedom she experienced and embraced as a follower of Jesus. In essence, she was free to be generous because of her deep and abiding knowledge of Jesus as her Savior and Lord.

Both of these women discovered their dignity in the context of their relationship with Christ. So when we are weary or worn out from praying—when our own wells have run dry from despair or depression or monotony—Jesus will call us to the deep well of his own heart. Whether we encounter Jesus disguised as our crying children, demanding parents, irritable husbands, or competitive coworkers, he asks us as he did the Samaritan woman, "Will you give me a drink?" What will we say? How can we be assured that we will respond with generosity and a selfless spirit?

AT THE LORD'S HAND

One powerful way we can respond with generosity is to embrace the role of handmaid, where our souls are *empty of self* and...*self-contained.*[108] At first glance, this might seem like a contradiction. Yet Edith is talking about emptying oneself of the web of agitation and preoccupation that so many of us are caught up in. Many times, our relationships with others can ensnare and deplete us and pull us away from that place of balance and peace that is ours at the Lord's hand.

God created woman to experience her complete fulfillment by giving herself generously to others, but sometimes she can find herself at odds with the culture and become confused by the tensions created when she gives herself away to the wrong people, under the wrong circumstances. This misguided surrender can cause deep wounding and pain, for even though surrender is the spiritual expression of the handmaid, it must be a purified surrender. To achieve this, Edith reminds us:

> We can do nothing ourselves; God must do it…[and once woman has] realized that no one other than God is capable of *receiving* her *completely* for Himself and that it is a sinful theft toward God to give oneself completely to one other than Him, then the surrender is no longer difficult and she becomes free of herself…. Now she has all that she needs; she reaches out when she is sent, and…she is ready as handmaid for all whom the Lord desires her to serve.[109]

Edith embraced this spiritual vision of handmaid for herself. In ancient times, a handmaid literally functioned as an extension of her lord or lady's hand. She positioned herself at the foot of her master and focused all of her attention on the task of carrying out the will or desire that was expressed. A handmaid was considered useful, even indispensable, when she was able to anticipate, out of familiarity and devotion, the will of her master. Edith articulated this role of handmaid as "living at the Lord's hand," and it was a consistent theme on which she spoke and upon which she took up her daily tasks. She said, "Whether she is a mother in the home or occupies a place in the limelight of public life, or lives behind quiet cloister walls, she must be a *handmaid of the Lord* everywhere."[110]

Are you beginning to get stirred up by the Holy Spirit to see the rich wisdom and perfect freedom that comes from embracing our feminine genius and the wonderful attributes that flow from it? Next, we will look at our God-given sensitivity as one more gift and expression of our genius.

POINTS TO PONDER

1. Reflect upon Edith's words when she says:

   Only God can welcome a person's total surrender in such a way that one does not lose one's soul in the process but wins it.[111]

   What are some examples from your own life that reflect this statement? How have you won your soul through surrender to God? If you haven't, what gets in the way of your soul's surrender?

2. What is the "living water" you need from Jesus? Through prayer and meditation on the story of the woman at the well, allow Jesus to draw you into a heart-to-heart conversation. Record in your journal what he says to you.

3. Think of the ways in which you count the cost in your life. Reflect on the ways the roles of handmaid and helpmate can help you to become more generous in these areas.

• chapter five •

Sensitivity: Feeding Our Souls

"The strength of woman lies in the emotional life."

How many times have you been told that you are too emotional or too sensitive? As women, we may have received the message that expressing our emotions is a weakness and that we need to be more stoic or logical in our approach to life's circumstances. Yet God gave us our emotions and sensitive natures as gifts to be delighted in and shared. The fabric of our feminine souls is stitched together with the vibrant and colorful emotions we use to express our inner lives. In fact, as our friend Edith confirms in the quote above, our strength "lies in our emotional life."[112]

Emotions are an essential part of what it means to be human. Jesus is our example and model. As an emotional Savior, he cried several times that we know of during his public ministry and expressed anger, joy, anguish, sorrow, and love—emotions we all share. As Edith explains, "the soul perceives its own being in the stirrings of the emotions. Through the emotions, it comes to know what it is and how it is; it also grasps through them the relationship of another being to itself…and the significance of the inherent value of exterior things, of unfamiliar people and impersonal things."[113]

MEN AND WOMEN HE MADE THEM

Given what Edith says, we can see that our emotions serve an important spiritual purpose. In fact, she says, "the emotions have been seen as the center of woman's soul…. It is only the person who is deeply involved with life whose emotions are stirred."[114] And we women are often deeply involved in the lives of others, much differently than men are. I'm always reminded of this fact when my husband comes home from going on errands without me.

From time to time, he will come back from his errand and tell me that he has run into someone, a friend or an acquaintance, that we haven't seen in a while. Naturally, I will then proceed to bombard him with all kinds of questions like: How are the kids? Did Jack find a job yet? Is Mary still taking care of her mother? And, inevitably, he will look back at me with a blank stare and say, " I don't know…I didn't ask." To which I will reply with incredulity, "What did you talk about then?" And he will simply say, "I don't really remember." My husband is not relationship-oriented, as I am, and isn't the least bit interested in whether little Susie got her braces off. It's not that he doesn't care; it is just that he is not wired that way. He's in the here and now, focusing intently on one practical matter at a time, devotedly single-minded and superbly equipped to hunt and protect, but not to remember details that to him are neither interesting nor necessary.

I, on the other hand, am emotionally invested in relationships and looking at the whole picture and the whole person and wanting the whole story of what is going on! As a woman, I am wired to want to know everything about everybody so that I can launch into fix-it mode. This scenario, repeated often, is proof positive that God has a sense of humor.

What we have come to understand in the secular culture about the differences between the sexes can be supported by what Edith describes as the distinctive nature or spiritual attitudes of men and women. In essence, "man is consumed by 'his enterprise'...generally it is difficult for him to become involved in other beings and their concerns. On the contrary, it is natural for woman...to interest herself empathically in areas of knowledge far from her own concerns."[115]

In fact, a great deal of Edith's writings focused on the differences between the natures of men and women that can help us to better understand the value of our sensitivity. We could probably boil it down into one sentence by saying, "Men are interested in things, and women are interested in people." This is not to take away from the beautiful complexities and dignity of the human person, but it gets to the heart of the matter and helps us to understand—and maybe to be a bit more patient with—the males in our lives. Additionally, we could say that man is a specialist and woman is a generalist. Edith states it like this: "Through submission to a discipline, man easily experiences a *one-sided development*. In woman, there lies a natural drive towards *totality* and *self-containment*."[116]

So what does all this mean? It means that we women feel and experience the world with the whole of our beings. We learn about ourselves and others through our emotions, and men learn by actions and accomplishments. While we make sense of the world and our experiences by viewing them as a whole or the sum of its parts, men make sense of the world and its challenges by breaking things down and conquering or analyzing the parts to determine a solution. Men compartmentalize while women embrace the whole.

The beauty of Edith's insight lies in the wisdom of the natural law and the way God created us to be complementary to one another. As a result, she has concluded that these gender differences are due to distinctive and permanent categories of male and female species that do not change—nor does the dignity ascribed to either ever diminish.

It's interesting to note that while Pope John Paul II, in his reflections collectively referred to as the Theology of the Body, references distinctions between males and females, he places less emphasis on the differences between men and women and more on the commonalities of our respective vocations. He emphasizes that "in the 'unity of the two,' man and woman are called from the beginning not only to exist 'side by side' or 'together,' but they are also called *to exist mutually 'one for the other'*.... To be human means to be called to interpersonal communion.[117]

In his *Letter to Women*, Pope John Paul II relayed his thoughts on male-female complementarity:

> The creation of woman is thus marked from the outset by *the principle of help:* a help which is not one-sided but *mutual.* Woman complements man, just as man complements woman: men and women are *complementary.* Womanhood expresses the "human" as much as manhood does, but in a different and complementary way.
>
> When the Book of Genesis speaks of "help," it is not referring merely to *acting,* but also to *being.* Womanhood and manhood are complementary *not only from the physical and psychological points of view,* but also from the *ontological.* It is only through the duality of the "masculine" and the "feminine'" that the "human" finds full realization.[118]

I know Edith would agree with John Paul II's assertion that "as a rational and free being, man is called to transform the face of the earth...*man and woman alike* share equal responsibility from the start."[119] The world needs our distinctive and complementary influences, starting within the small circle of the family and rippling out into the community and the world.

BLESSED BALANCE

Woman's special sensitivity needs to be purified and submitted to the effects of grace, lest she fall into what Edith refers to as stark carnality or undue sensuality, allowing her sensitive nature to get the upper hand over her intellect and will. With our gift of sensitivity and our emotions at the seat of our souls, we can see why we should put forth the effort and energy to exercise emotional prudence and seek emotional chastity in our daily lives in the way that God intended. It's important for us to understand the way we are called to integrate our emotions for our good and the good of others. Balance is the key here.

Edith warns against unilateral emotional development because emotional stirrings need the control of reason and the direction of the will. Where discipline of mind and will are lacking, emotional life becomes a compulsion without secure direction. We become at risk of addiction to sensuality and a decline of spiritual life.[120]

It is precisely because we are at risk of distortion and imbalance in our emotional lives that Edith concludes that "the nature and destiny of woman require an education which can inspire works of effective love…and therefore…emotional training is the most important factor required in the formation of woman;…such authentic formation is related to intellectual clarity and energy as well as to practical competence."[121]

I don't want to dwell on the negative here because there is so much that is beautiful and right and good about women's sensitivity. Yet, in order for us to embrace the genius of our sensitivity, we need to be able to examine the ways in which this blessing of sensitivity can become a curse, so to speak. Edith talks about two specifically.

One way is that this gift can become exaggerated and distorted, causing women to become one-sided. In this, "abstract thought and creative action are of less concern to her than the possession and enjoyment of the good life.... [As a result], her reverent joy in the things of this world may degenerate into greed...and hoarding of things for which she has no use; and...a lapse into a mindless, idle life of sensuality."[122]

Within our family relationships, this imbalance can lead to possessiveness and cause a woman to

> hover anxiously over her children as if they were her own possessions [and lead her] to bind her to them in every way, even by the greatest possible elimination of the father's rights. She will try to curtail their freedom of development; she will check their development and destroy their happiness instead of serving man, children, and all creatures in a reverential and loving manner.[123]

In this reflection, Edith seems to be painting the portrait of the overbearing wife or mother. It may seem like a stereotype, but it can be traced back to original sin and chalked up to concupiscence. It's valuable for us to make the connection between our sensitive natures and our propensity to dominate and take control in our relationships with others, especially with our husbands and our children. Armed with self-knowledge and calling upon grace, we can rise above this potential weakness.

The same holds true for the second result of a disordered sensitivity. This is when we fall prey to a hypersensitivity that renders us touchy and easily offended. (Does this sound familiar, ladies?) This happens because we can become too attached to what other people think or feel about us and we overreact in a way that is indicative of our inclination to vanity and desire for praise, recognition, and attention. (Ouch!)

For the better part of my life, my emotions ruled. They had the capacity to define my day and my world when I let them. More often than not, they led me to grumbling and unhealthy comparisons with others. But living our lives by emotion is like building our houses on shifting sand; there is no foundation! As a result of this in my own life, I was insecure and defensive most of the time—and truly unhappy. No matter how hard I tried to get things under control, and I did try, I still seemed to be deeply affected by shifting and intense emotions.

Maybe you find yourself in the same boat? Or perhaps you have gone the opposite route and stifled your emotions to the point of a rigidity that has yielded an overall apathy for life. Has your God-given gift of sensitivity gone astray in your life? Let me assure you that there is a remedy for this. Edith reminds us that it is "only by the power of grace [that nature can] be liberated from its dross, restored to purity and made free to receive divine life."[124]

Through prayer and God's grace, we are called to seek a purification of our emotions. Here's an exercise that helped me. First, identify the dominant emotion that is your fallback whenever things get tough. It may be anger, fear, or sadness. Perhaps it is suspicion, a sense of worthlessness, or rejection. It is any habitual emotional reaction that you have experienced for a very long time that has led you into a pattern of behavior that is self-defeating when you are relating to others.

For me, the emotion was fear. It was my reaction to just about everything, and it caused me to be demanding in relationships, especially with my husband. I tried to control everything because I was afraid of what would happen if I didn't. It was a learned reaction left over from childhood and it wasn't making me a very productive adult. Edith's declaration that this oversensitivity is something quite common in women, and something that she herself experienced and dealt with, gave me great confidence and hope for change and balance. For whatever your damaging emotions are, they can be transformed and transforming when received as a great gift from God!

Once you have identified the emotion that is out of balance, the next step is to find a Scripture verse that directly addresses that emotion. I found two to combat my sense of fear: "For God did not give us a spirit of timidity but a spirit of power and love and self-control" (2 Timothy 1:7) and "Create in me a clean heart, O God, / and put a new and right spirit within me" (Psalm 51:10). Work with these passages to lead your heart in a healthy direction. I repeated these verses every day and meditated upon them every night for a year. Every time fear and anxiety crept into my spirit, I would say the verses to myself. You can do the same thing for any area or situation in your life where you are hypersensitive.

Over the course of that year, balance was restored to my emotions, and I began to experience less fear and more joy, gratitude, and peace. I also became less hypersensitive and more confident. The Good News means that we can cooperate with God's grace for our emotions by conducting a good examination of our motives, making it a goal to rise above our desire to have everyone like and approve of us, and doing our own work to put our emotions and sensitivities in their rightful place.

Today's world presents us with another challenge when it comes to our emotions. Many of us may be at risk of an emotional overload, whereby we experience desensitization to all the things happening around us. Instead of feeling empathy, we just grow numb to the bad things that are happening to others. Far from being sensitive or feeling deeply, we find ourselves on emotional autopilot to preserve and protect ourselves against our repeated exposure to the difficulties and real horror others are facing around the world, or even in our own backyards.

While the television and the Internet magnify the brutality of this world for us in ways that Edith could not have imagined, it was she who came face-to-face with the real horrors of her time in the form of the Nazi occupation and persecution of her people. Still, she remained emotionally connected and retained emotional engagements of the heart that surely caused her great pain. One glimpse of this comes from one of her students who said:

> Edith Stein was often merry and cheerful like a child, but mostly serious and thoughtful. Especially when the persecution of the Jews began, she got more and more grave when she thought of her family. You never heard her complain, but it was shattering to see her quiet face, drawn with pain. Already her features showed a glimmer of the mystery that was expressed in her religious name, "of the Cross."[125]

This way of the cross Edith embraced, took on as part of her name, and championed in her life and by her death, gives us an example of how to live without losing our emotional connection in times such as ours. Edith spoke of this in a prayerful conversation she had with Jesus: "I talked with the Savior, and told Him that I knew that it was His cross that was now being placed upon the Jewish people; that most of them did not understand this; but that those who did, would have to take it up willingly in the name of all. I would do that. He should only show me how."[126] Lord, help us to have this same kind of courage; to remain sensitive in the face of suffering and follow your footsteps wherever they may lead!

THE SOURCE OF OUR EMOTIONAL STRENGTH

The divine life of Christ is uniquely expressed and reflected by a woman's disciplined and purified emotions. Thanks be to God, we can go to him for help. As Edith discovered and declared:

For every Catholic there lies ready an immeasurable treasure: the proximity of the Lord in the holy sacrifice and in the most holy sacrament of the altar. Whoever is imbued with a lively faith in Christ present in the tabernacle, whoever knows that a friend awaits here constantly—always with the time, patience, and sympathy to listen to complaints, petitions, and problems with counsel and help in all things—this person cannot remain desolate and forsaken even under the greatest difficulties. He always has a refuge where *quietude and peace can again be found.*[127]

Edith's relationship with Jesus in the Eucharist completely engaged her person: mind, body, soul, and *emotions*. She offered all to him as a total gift of self, and through that donation, she enjoyed a holy intimacy with Christ that is revealed in an excerpt from one of her poems:

This Heart, it beats for us in a small tabernacle
Where is remains mysteriously hidden
In that still, white host.
That is your royal throne on earth, O Lord....
Full of love, you sink your gaze into mine.[128]

How marvelous it is that the beautiful gift of our emotions feeds our souls with an intuitive knowledge and strength that have the great capacity and purpose to inform and influence the world for the better. The treasures of our feminine sensitivity, in concert with the blessings that flow from the Holy Eucharist, bring about an inner awareness that is foundational to an innate maternal wisdom. This wisdom, as we will find out, is not limited to a physical or biological maternity, but extends to a spiritual one in us all. In the next chapter, we'll explore this gift of maternity and its relation to our universal and eternal call as women— our vocation of love.

POINTS TO PONDER

1. How do you feel about the gift of your emotions? Are your emotions like friends or foes? What changes can you make to bring balance to your emotions?

2. Reflect upon Edith's observation that as women we can fall prey to "a mania to know everything." Does this resonate with you? How does it play out in your life and your relationships with others?

3. Write a vow or prayer to Jesus, as your Eucharistic Savior, to place him at the center of your heart and emotional life.

· *chapter six* ·

Maternity: Our Vocation of Love

"Filled with the spirit of supernatural maternity, woman has the
mission to win others over as children of God."

I'll never forget the day my daughter was born. After twenty-one hours of
hard labor (yes, all labor is hard!), I was gifted with a precious little
bundle of love who was completely dependent on me, but at the same
time had the power to change my entire life and the tenor of my heart
with one tiny gurgle. For nine months, I had been nurturing her spirit
and nourishing her body in the mysterious and hidden haven of my
womb. I felt an inexplicable bond with her from the moment of my
awareness of her conception, and on that day, I was finally able to meet
the little soul whom God had created and entrusted to my husband
and me.

Beyond the love and joy I felt that day was an experience that I wasn't
quite expecting and one I will never forget. Late in the evening of my
daughter's birthday, after my family had gone home, I was left alone
to contemplate with wonder the extraordinary miracle of that day. As
any mother would be, I was eager to hold my baby, so I walked down
the dimly lit hall toward the nursery. As I did, I was filled with an
overwhelming sense of empowerment and strength. I felt a deep and
life-defining sense of accomplishment I had never known before—
and haven't since. It was a soul-stirring flicker of connection with all

mothers who had gone before me. I felt an inspired sense of solidarity with them in the accomplishment of God's sublime purpose to create life. I also felt as though I could have taken on the world with the fierce and unconquerable love welling up within me for my child. In short, everything I felt in those fleeting moments culminated in an affirmation that I had just cooperated in the most validating experience of my life.

I believe what I experienced on that day was what Edith refers to in the quote above as the "spirit of supernatural maternity." This experience is not limited to biological motherhood, as Edith repeatedly points out, for "*to be a mother* is to nourish and protect true humanity and bring it to development."[129] This precious gift of maternity is the primary calling of all women and is our deepest fulfillment. It brings us into direct connection with our eternal purpose, and we are sublimely equipped to carry out this maternal mission in all our encounters with others.

Our world is searching, striving, and starving for the authentic feminine expression of what Edith calls *motherliness* and what Pope John Paul II referred to as the *genius of women* and *affective, cultural, and spiritual motherhood.*[130] As women, we are bound by a divine obligation to explore this gift in the deepest way possible, to ponder and reflect upon our maternal roles, and to embrace the call in our lives of this beautiful and rich feminine vocation. We are called to nurture and nourish humanity and to "preserve the deep intuition of the goodness in [our] lives of those actions which elicit life, and contribute to the growth and protection of the other."[131] It just doesn't get any more beautiful than that!

A VOCATION AT RISK

Unfortunately, motherhood seems to be in crisis, and woman's maternal vocation is under attack. Many people trace the origins of this degradation of the role of mother and breakdown of the family to the feminist movement of the 1960s and 1970s in this country. There is no doubt that it has taken a huge toll on women's relationships with themselves and with their husbands and children. It seems clear that the chaos and confusion of roles—and woman's ensuing ambivalence about motherhood—can be directly attributed to the rise in popularity of this movement. So we have to ask the question: Is the quality of women's lives better or worse because of it?

This is not to say that the feminist movement is entirely to blame for our current state of affairs, because it did not proliferate in a vacuum. In addition, some very positive things came from it. In fact, Edith makes a comparison between the Catholic Woman's Movement of her day and the secular women's movement—a movement that started out with admirable and high ideals but was, in a sense, taken over by "forceful power factions...[that caused] the movement [to be] crushed by new ideology, in the universities as well as in political life."[132]

We have seen the same thing happen in our country in recent times, where the admirable principles of the original suffragettes and early feminist movements have been co-opted by the self-serving and political agendas of abortion rights activists and organizations such as Planned Parenthood. In response, what Edith referred to as the Catholic Woman's Movement has seen resurgence and is now called the New Feminism or Authentic Feminism. It has also blossomed in response to Pope John Paul II's call for the faithful to build a culture of life and a civilization of love. His apostolic letters and encyclicals dedicated to the topic of women's issues are based largely on Edith's writings and have energized and inspired a whole new generation of Catholic women. Both Catholic movements, then and now, hold the same ideals in opposition to the secular feminist ones. Edith explains:

Our guiding star is not the liberal ideal of humanity and femininity conditioned by time. Rather, our ideal is one which exists prior to all time and which will endure for all time. Woman is created by God to stand by her husband's side; to stand with him over and above all other creatures; she is bound to him as the helpmate who corresponds to him in an enduring, indissoluble coexistence. They are charged—and the woman is in more specific ways—to beget and rear children not only in strength, health, and fitness for life but as citizens of God's kingdom.[133]

Essentially, Edith and today's Catholic feminists are confirming that woman's power lies in her gift of maternity, both physical and spiritual. Through Edith's teachings and example and through the birth and life of my own daughter, I have learned how important it is for us to grasp the profound gift maternity brings to bear upon the entire world and the need to protect and preserve it as a God-given spiritual gift of every woman.

The fact remains that the liberation of women around the world is still incomplete. There are countless women, especially in developing countries, who are considered second-class citizens and who suffer indignities and inequalities of every sort. Again in his *Letter to Women*, Pope John Paul II pointed this out when he wrote:

Women's dignity has often been unacknowledged and their prerogatives misrepresented; they have often been relegated to the margins of society and even reduced to servitude. This has prevented women from truly being themselves and it has resulted in a spiritual impoverishment of humanity.[134]

Currently, the world's response to the plight of these women, through the United Nations and on an international level, has been to provide them with free (sometimes forced) sterilizations and massive amounts of birth control. It is thought that to emancipate woman from her vocation of motherhood will somehow end the exploitation, bringing dignity to her cause and equity to her life. Nothing could be further from the truth. These anti-life actions not only violate God's law, but the laws of common sense and decency, as well. For these reasons and more, we must continue to put forth an authentic feminism that champions the real rights and essential dignity of women.

The culture of death's full frontal attack upon women's maternity works to devalue every human life that women are uniquely equipped to champion and protect. Knowing how vital our maternal mission is to the world, it is no wonder that evil has found its way into the sanctuary of the woman's womb and endeavored to destroy the fruits thereof. So many women are ignorant of their supreme vocation of physical and spiritual motherhood. Nevertheless, where there is knowledge, there is hope—tremendous hope that we can discover our true genius and our intrinsic and integral value as women in our world today.

A VOCATION IS BORN

Edith's *Essays on Woman* seem to be so directly foundational to the writings and works of Pope John Paul II's Theology of the Body that the two are like inseparable companions. Together, these two intellectual and spiritual powerhouses have transformed our understanding of human dignity in the context of a worldwide culture that is hell-bent on self-destruction. They are, in the fullest sense of the words, *prophets of life* who have provided us with a body of knowledge that can lead to a rich and transcendent self-understanding that calls upon women to embrace our potential and exercise our responsibility to "aid humanity in not falling."[135]

For me, this discovery was made possible through the *Essays on Woman*. I was so in the dark about what it meant to be a woman that I fell prey to the whole self-aggrandizing agenda of the feminist movement by the time I was seventeen years old. The Church did her best to teach me the truth, but this was the 1970s, during the height of the bra-burning era of Betty Freidan, the proliferation of contraception, and the almost immediate confusion between the sexes that resulted. The chaos in our culture seemed to catch fire at this time in the cauldron of discontent that was fueled by a culture-wide clamoring for equal rights for women, inside and outside of the bedroom.

By the time I left for college, I had left the Catholic Church. I would not return until I had endured years of infertility and was pregnant with my first and, as it turned out, only living child after suffering three miscarriages. Finding my way back was a miracle, second only to the one I was carrying inside of me at the time. I was confused and terrified about being a mother—and equally apprehensive about the Catholic Church. Yet something was calling me back, and I now know that something was a someone, in the form of the Holy Spirit. Thanks be to God, I was welcomed back with open arms.

Very soon thereafter, I read the *Essays on Woman* and embarked on a journey of self-discovery. I learned what it means to be a mother and woman in the fullest and most complete sense of those esteemed roles. As you clearly know by now, learning these lessons from Edith has been life-changing and life-defining for me in the best way possible. She showed me the value of seeking formation for my soul and developing a self-knowledge so that I can, in turn, share her wisdom with others, especially girls and women. Writing this book is the culmination of all those valuable lessons!

MARY IS OUR MODEL

By now I hope you understand that a spiritual maternity is your calling, too, no matter what your state in life. And while many women will never know physical motherhood, all women have a connection to motherhood because all women have a mother: a biological or earthly one and a spiritual one. Many women, however, because of a difficult relationship with their own mothers, have a hard time relating to the Blessed Mother. I know this was the case for me, and I have met more than a few women who have indicated the same dynamic in their lives. This is both understandable and rectifiable.

In my case, I had to lay aside some of my past hurts and push through some of my fears about not being lovable or good enough. As I slowly prayed my way through these difficult wounds from my earthly mother, I found myself turning more and more to Mary when I needed spiritual help or intercession. I started to devote more time to Mary during prayer and thought about her more during each day. As I got to know her, I began to trust her more and more and sought to be more like her. This will be a lifelong journey as I continue to discover more of the mystery of her grace and the depth of her motherly love.

If there is need for healing, forgiveness, or reconciliation in your relationship with your earthly mother, Mary can help. Contemplate her role at the wedding at Cana, when she stepped forth boldly and firmly and approached her Son to solve the problem of a lack of wine. Her role was undeniably that of intercessor. She was the mediator: the one who approached him and would not let him off the hook without action. That was just a simple matter of saving some people from embarrassment, so imagine the depth of her pleading when it comes to the reconciliation of her children with one another. There is nothing that matters more to a mother's heart than having her children get along! If you want a stronger connection to Jesus, go through Mary. She never gets tired of interceding, and he cannot deny her!

If you are one of the fortunate ones who have always known the love, comfort, and guidance of the Blessed Mother in your life, then perhaps you will be called upon to reflect and reveal that grace to others. Don't miss the opportunity to do so. Certainly, you already know the power of your prayers to Mary and the efficacious manner in which we are aided by her Holy and Immaculate heart. Always be ready to share with others the truth—that she is a perfect Mother and model and that it is through her that we learn the gift of our spiritual maternity and what it is to be a woman in the likeness and image of God.

There is a deep richness to the lives of those who strive to imitate Mary. However, many people, especially women, find her perfection intimidating. This was another reason why I had kept Mary at a distance—because of my own insecurity, pride, and prejudice against her. I felt I could never be as good as Mary, so why should I try? I fell prey to that sin of comparison that stems from the root sin of vanity. Yet the hallmark of Mary's example is humility. In humility, a woman ultimately forgets herself; forgets both her shortcomings and accomplishments equally and strives to remain empty of self to make room for Jesus, just as Mary did.

Pope John Paul II, like many Church leaders and saints before him, believed that the surest way to the heart of Jesus is through Mary and that the shortest route to her heart is to pray the rosary. It is essential for women in our day to know who Mary is and what her mission is in this world. We are in the Marian age, and Mary's presence is needed to "crush the head of the serpent." Her influence will be known in the world through women who emulate her. Edith believed, and Pope John Paul II reinforced the belief, that God will combat evil in our day through the power of maternal love and through women who follow the example of Our Blessed Mother. Here's what Edith said:

The Mother of God is among all women the most intimately bound to Christ; she is the heart of the Church of which Christ is the head. Her singular support gladdens all women who want to be mothers in this supernatural sense. For just as Mary begot total humanity in Christ through her offspring—"Be it done unto me according to Thy will"—just so does she help those who strive to unveil Christ in the heart of another. Thus, woman's mission is to imitate Mary.[136]

And Pope John Paul II said in his *Letter to Women*:

> *The Church sees in Mary the highest expression of the "feminine genius"* and she finds in her a source of constant inspiration. Mary called herself the "handmaid of the Lord" (*Lk* 1:38). Through obedience to the Word of God she accepted her lofty yet not easy vocation as wife and mother in the family of Nazareth. Putting herself at God's service, she also put herself at the service of others: a *service of love*. Precisely through this service Mary was able to experience in her life a mysterious, but authentic "reign." It is not by chance that she is invoked as "Queen of heaven and earth." The entire community of believers thus invokes her; many nations and peoples call upon her as their "Queen." *For her, "to reign" is to serve! Her service is "to reign"!*[137]

Now we can see how vital woman's mission and reign of service is to the world and how Mary is our model. Mary is a genuine and dynamic mother to us all. As Edith states:

> The title of Mary as our mother is not merely symbolic. Mary is our mother in the most real and lofty sense which surpasses that of earthly maternity. She begot our life of grace for us because she offered up her entire being, body and soul' as the Mother of God.
>
> That is why an intimate bond exists between Mary and ourselves. She loves us, she know us, she exerts herself to bring each one of us into the closest possible relationship with the Lord—that which we are above all supposed to be.[138]

Reading Edith's words about Mary reveals that she truly embraced Mary and came to know and rely upon her as the Mother who dwelled within her heart. She encourages that same kind of personal relationship with Mary for all of us. Edith gives us a beautiful portrait and analogy to describe the potential for this relationship when she writes:

> Just as the heart sustains the other organs of woman's body and makes it possible for them to function, so we may genuinely believe there is just such a collaboration of Mary with every woman wherever that woman is fulfilling her vocation.[139]

Edith also reminds us that:

> Just as grace cannot achieve its work in souls unless they open themselves to it in free decision, so also Mary cannot function fully as a mother if people do not entrust themselves to her…if they also entrust themselves to her guidance and place themselves completely under her care. She herself can form in her own image those who belong to her.[140]

Isn't it the greatest blessing that we have such a mother? Have you ever considered this call to collaboration with the Blessed Mother? Can you think of ways in which you can more actively place your trust in Mary's guidance and care? Just imagine our society when every woman understands her dignity, value, and true nature as it is reflected in Mary—and uses her gifts and feminine genius to transform the world!

THE MOTHER IN US ALL

If there is anything we can learn from Edith, it is that we women are responsible for educating ourselves and then sharing all we learn about the truth of our vocation with other girls and women to promote, affirm, and encourage the essential role of motherhood (both physical and spiritual) for the good of ourselves, our families, and our world.

She describes this maternal mission and calls woman "to war against evil and to educate her posterity to do the same; this has been true of woman including the Mother of the Son who conquered death and hell, but it will have to remain so until the end of the world."[141]

Edith refers to the educated and enlightened woman as "a pillar which many can fasten themselves, thereby attaining a firm footing." She claims that "when women themselves are once again whole persons and when they help others to become so, they create healthy, energetic spores supplying healthy energy to the entire national body."[142] Of physical motherhood, she describes mothers who

> have a firm philosophy of life, who know to *what purpose* they should rear their children, who have an open vision of the developmental possibilities of their children. But also who have an incorruptible perspective of the dangerous drives in them which must be curtailed and which must be seized with a powerful hand at the right moment.[143]

And prophetically for our times, Edith adds the following:

> And these also must be mothers who know their place, who do not think that they are able to do everything themselves but, on the contrary, are able to let go of their children and place them in God's hand when the time comes, when the children have outgrown them.[144]

These are powerful and very wise statements that give clear snapshots of what motherhood is all about. They paint a picture of a strong motherly influence that guides the moral and spiritual development of her children. They are words—refreshingly honest and forthright— that inspire and speak to the great and arduous task that motherhood presents. As any mother will tell you, motherhood is the most difficult job in the world! It is also the most rewarding, of course, and a true vocation, for it will teach and stretch the mother even more than the child. Many mothers will say they are better human beings because of their children and the roles each one has played in their lives.

Perhaps it is fitting that I am finishing the last draft of this chapter on the occasion of my seventeenth Mother's Day. In light of that, early this morning, I ran across a beautiful passage from Pope John Paul II that I knew was meant to be included in this book. It reads:

> Motherhood involves a special communion with the mystery of life as it develops in the woman's womb. The mother is filled with wonder at this mystery of life and "understands" with unique intuition what is happening inside her. In the light of the "beginning," the mother accepts and loves as a person the child she is carrying in her womb. This unique contact with the new human being developing within her gives rise to an attitude toward human beings—not only towards her own child, but every human being—which profoundly marks the woman's personality. It is commonly thought that *women* are more capable than men of paying attention *to another person* and that motherhood develops this predisposition even more. The man—even with all his sharing in parenthood—always remains "outside" the process of pregnancy and the baby's birth; in many ways he has to *learn* his own *"fatherhood" from the mother*.... The mother's contribution is decisive in laying the foundation for a new human personality.[145]

THE GIFT OF SPIRITUAL MOTHERHOOD

Mother, mentor, teacher: These three roles all make up what Edith calls woman's supernatural maternity. Even though many women may be confused about the role of motherhood today, we can help them find their way. For those women who deny the wisdom of the Church that ascribes such dignity to every woman, we can educate them and steer them away from the counterfeit, superficial, and worldly forms of perfection that are damaging and rejecting of woman's core value and unique destiny as mother. Reflecting on this gift of maternity, Edith invites us to embrace the role of teacher to further the life of faith by providing a secure and enduring foundation and be the "maternal, loving educator for Christ."[146]

The role of mentor is for every woman, at any age or stage in her life. This aspect of spiritual motherhood is reflected in this description from Edith. She relates that

> woman's intrinsic value can work in every place and thereby institute grace…. Everywhere she meets with a human being, she will find opportunity to sustain, to counsel, to help…. Everywhere the need exists for maternal sympathy and help…we are able to recapitulate in the *one* word *motherliness*… that which does not remain within the narrow circle of blood relations or personal friends; but in accordance with the model of the Mother of Mercy…must have its root in universal divine love for all who are there, belabored and burdened.[147]

I have been doubly blessed in my life by the presence of two such spiritual mothers: Mary and Alice. Neither woman had children of her own, but both became surrogate mothers, mentors, and teachers for me when I was a child. They provided a safe haven and sweet refreshment for my soul. Mary was my babysitter, and she is the Mary after whom I named my own daughter. From the time that I was six years old until I was in my late teens, Mary extended tenderness and a nurturing acceptance that sustained me through some difficult times. She also taught me many practical things, like how to write cursive and how to talk with an accent like Julia Child! Mary made a beautiful and lasting imprint on my life, and I can trace many of my motherly traits back to her. I still pray for her soul every night and joyfully await our happy meeting again one day in heaven!

Then there was Alice, my next-door neighbor when I was growing up. She had more wrinkles than anybody I had ever seen, but she was also the most beautiful lady I knew. She opened her home and her heart to me—and let me play in her garden, cook in her kitchen, and jump on her living room sofa. During the course of our time together, Alice extended warmth and hospitality toward me in a way that I had never experienced and will never forget. I pray for her soul, too, and she is no doubt part of my heavenly posse fulfilling the role of spiritual mother from on high.

These two women are entwined in the fabric of my heart. They brought Jesus and his life and example to me in the form of big bear hugs, a warm cozy kitchen, endless glasses of chocolate milk, and side-splitting laughter. I would not be the woman that I am today without their presence and influence in my life, as I learned to love from the love they showed to me. We must *never* underestimate the motherly role we can play and the impact we can have on others' hearts, minds, and lives.

Katrina Zeno is a writer and teacher on topics relating to women and the Theology of the Body and cofounder of the Women of the Third Millennium. In her article entitled, "Why Woman?" she provides a definition of spiritual motherhood as "nurturing the emotional, moral, cultural, and spiritual lives of others." As she says:

> This means women can be spiritual mothers anywhere: At the grocery store, in the office, working in the fields, even flat in bed. When a woman makes a meal for a friend, gives someone a spiritual book, prays the rosary, provides a listening ear, or monitors what her children watch on TV, she's nurturing the emotional, moral, cultural, and spiritual lives of others.[148]

Ultimately, women's maternity bears fruit when we carry Christ to others; when we give birth to the life of Christ in all of our encounters. My first book, *Refresh Me, Lord!*, contains a reflection entitled, "Life Bearers for Christ," in which I wrote that "women are called to be life bearers in many different ways. We are created to bring forth life, not just physically, but emotionally, spiritually, and artistically, as well. Just like Mary, who bore Life himself, we have the capacity to bring glory to God and to magnify his goodness" with every one we meet.[149]

IT'S ALL ABOUT LOVE

Women, we have a beautiful service and vocation of love to share with the world! And yes, it truly is all about love! When Mary said yes to life, she said yes to love, and it is the same with us. When we surrender to the Holy Spirit, as she did, and remain open to receiving life and the light of Christ in our hearts, we will fulfill our vocation and greatest potential as women. Though speaking of religious life here, Edith's meaningful words pertain to all of us:

> The motive, principle, and goal…is to surrender to God entirely in self-forgetting love, allowing one's own life to end in order to make room in oneself for God's life.
>
> The more completely this is realized the more is the soul filled with the riches of divine life…. Divine life is love overflowing, undemanding love freely giving itself; love that in compassion bends down to every creature in need; love that heals the sick and awakens the dead to life; love that protects and shelters, nourishes, teaches and shapes us; love that mourns with the mourners, rejoices with the joyful, and puts itself at the service of every creature so that each creature may become what the Father wishes it to be—in a word: the love of the Divine Heart.[150]

Self-forgetting…undemanding…freely given love.

POINTS TO PONDER

1. Reflect upon your relationships with your earthly mother and the Blessed Mother. Are there areas in need of healing or reconciliation? What are they? Take them to prayer and ask for Mary's intercession.

2. How can you cultivate or expand upon spiritual maternity in your current roles and responsibilities as wife, mother, sister, coworker, friend?

3. In what ways can you collaborate with Mary to fulfill your vocation as a woman in the Body of Christ?

"The nation...doesn't simply need what we have.
It needs what we are."

There has been a certain sense of urgency in my heart as I have written this book. After the completion of each chapter, I felt an ever-strengthening stirring deep within that confirmed my desire to share my spiritual friendship with Edith with you so that you can know her, too. But beyond that, I have been firmly guided by a growing confidence in the conviction that Edith's message is ripe for the season that women are in, right here...right now.

Simply put: We need her wisdom and example. The world is in desperate need of women who understand their inherent value and dignity; faith-filled women who are prepared to shape the world and influence the direction of humanity by *who they are*. As Edith states, "[God] has called women in all times to the most intimate union with Him: they are to be emissaries of his love, proclaimers of His will to kings and popes, and forerunners of His Kingdom in the hearts of men.... [It] is the most sublime vocation which has been given, and whoever sees this way open before her will yearn for no other way."[151]

I hope that by coming to know Edith, you have also come to know yourself more fully and, of course, come closer to the Lord whom she knew and loved so dearly. Edith was guided by grace as her relationship with Christ grew, and this surrender to grace is the special prerogative and spiritual mission of every woman. Edith said, "What we can and must do is open ourselves to grace; that means to renounce our own will completely and to give it captive to the divine will, to lay our whole soul, ready for reception and formation, into God's hands."[152]

This dynamic receptivity of which she speaks has the potential to breathe new life into the whole world. The unique manner in which women were created to receive Jesus into their feminine souls is described by Edith as "God's call inviting them to dedicate all their faculties to Him, and if they follow this call, then their lives as women become full and fruitful."[153] I want my life to be fruitful, don't you?

One of the most profound and beautiful things that I believe Edith ever said, and perhaps the statement that best reflects the truth of her life, was that "surrender is the highest act of…freedom."[154] It was through this surrender that Edith found her greatest joy, her deepest love, and her true destiny as a saint. Reflecting upon the example of the saints and their surrender, Edith said:

> Where there is genuine, lively faith, there the doctrine of faith and the "tremendous deeds" of God are the content of life. All else steps aside for it and is determined by it. This is *holy realism*: the original inner receptivity of the soul reborn in the Holy Spirit. Whatever the soul encounters is received in an appropriate manner and with corresponding depth and finds within the soul a living, mobile, docile energy that allows itself to be easily and joyfully led and molded…with unimpaired vigor and vitality, and with uninhibited simplicity.[155]

These words are perfectly descriptive of Edith! In fact, reflecting upon her life, Edith said, "Things were in God's plan which I had not planned at all. I am coming to the living faith and conviction that—from God's point of view—there is no chance and that the whole of my life, down to every detail, has been mapped out in God's divine providence and makes complete and perfect sense in God's all-seeing eyes."[156] Edith grew in trust, intimacy, and knowledge of God and love of Jesus to the extent that she was willing to lovingly surrender and embrace his cross and follow him, even to her death, for the good and love of others. And by all accounts, she did so joyfully and with uninhibited simplicity.

A LOVING LEGACY

The legacy Edith leaves us is threefold. First, she has gifted us with a rich treasure trove of writings that help us to understand and embrace the beauty and dignity of our feminine souls. She speaks to all women of any generation because she speaks God's truth for the highest mission and purpose of women in his kingdom here on earth. This truth for women transcends the time and culture in which we live and springs forth from a dignity inscribed in the very depths of our being by our loving creator and Father God. It is an indelible and inalienable truth, but we must uncover the treasure and seek those who can help us glean its mystery and share its wealth.

Second, Edith extends a vital invitation through her writings and example. She calls us to teach other women and girls by consciously sharing the wisdom we gain through self-discovery and our relationship with Christ. Edith called this the second ideal: that the fruit of our devotion to our true mission and our commitment of love will ensure that we use our feminine genius to evangelize, in the purest sense of that word.

Pope Paul VI officially defined this type of evangelization as "bringing the Good News into all the strata of humanity, and through its influence, transforming humanity from within and making it new."[157] Elaborating on this foundation, Pope John Paul II spoke of a New Evangelization where "the faithful move from a faith of habit, sustained perhaps by social context alone, to a faith which is conscious and personally lived. The renewal of faith will always be the best way to lead others to the Truth that is Christ.[158] Edith simply said, "We need women who dedicate their lives to the purpose of educating youth, women who are fully aware of the teachings of the faith, and of its historical background. Their intent will be to form a generation which is happy in faith and strong in spirit."[159]

Third, Edith leaves for us a clear path to the cross. By her life and death, we are reassured and encouraged, just as we are by Christ, to *be not afraid* when our search for truth leads us to the foot of the cross. And according to Edith, it inevitably will, for she says "whoever belongs to Christ must go the whole way with him. He must mature to adulthood: he must one day or other walk the way of the cross to Gethsemane and Golgotha."[160]

It is natural for us to want to avoid the cross, as even Jesus asked for his Father to allow it to pass him by. And we can identify in our culture today a strong resistance to suffering—an avoidance of pain and inconvenience at all costs—but this is merely a hyperbole of fallen human nature. Perhaps because our foundational Christian ideals are being erased from society and replaced with an unrestrained hedonism, the decidedly Catholic Christian action of making reparation has fallen off the radar. On a personal and cultural level, we are confronted with mounting evidence that we are on the verge of a complete cutoff from the value of redemptive suffering and self-sacrifice or the offering up of one's comfort, or very life, for another.

This is so contrary to Edith's example, as one who lived up to her name and her own remarks when she said, "One cannot wish for a deliverance from the cross when one bears the noble title 'of the Cross.'"[161] The truth is that the cross will always remain a contradiction and mystery, so how can we overcome our natural tendencies to avoid suffering for a greater spiritual end? Edith explains that "only someone whose spiritual eyes to the supernatural correlations of worldly events can desire suffering in expiation, and this is only possible for people in whom the spirit of Christ dwells, who...are given life by the Lord, receive his power, his meaning, and his direction."[162]

Edith points to some examples of these cross-bearers who represent the ways in which we can offer ourselves and our suffering to God. She says that "the archetype of followers of the cross for all time is the Mother of God. Typical of those who submit to the suffering inflicted on them and experience his blessing by bearing it is Simon of Cyrene. Representative of those who love him and yearn to serve the Lord is Veronica."[163]

I'd like to add to Edith's list the wailing women whom Jesus also encounters on the Via Dolorosa. Jesus tells them not to weep for him, but for themselves and for their children. He foretells a time when people will be in great anguish (Is that time now?), and he invites the women to take up their plight. Once again, he is speaking to women exclusively and asking them (and us) to aid others, in a uniquely feminine way, to bear their burdens and carry their crosses. In fact, Edith points out that "the lovers of the cross whom [Jesus] has awakened and who will always continue to awaken anew in the changeable history of the struggling church [will be] his allies at the end of time. We, too, are called for that purpose."[164]

Those who are called and do become lovers of the cross will find that "voluntary expiatory suffering is what truly and really unites one to the Lord intimately...and...the love of the cross in no way contradicts being a joyful child of God. Helping Christ carry his cross fills one with a strong and pure joy, and those who may and can do so, the builders of God's kingdom, are the most authentic children of God."[165]

A SAINT FOR OUR TIMES

If Edith were alive today, I believe that she would be spending most of her time on her knees, before her Beloved in the Blessed Sacrament. She would be storming heaven with the strength of her prayers for the well-being of the whole world. While Edith wrote the following in 1933 just after she entered Carmel, she could just as easily say these words today about the power and need for prayer and devotion to the Blessed Sacrament, to which she was referring:

> While outside in carnival's frantic tumult people get drunk and delirious, while political battles separate them and great need depresses them so much that many forget to look to heaven, at such still places of prayer hearts are opened to the Lord…they offer him their warm love…. By their steadfast supplications, they draw down God's grace and mercy on a humanity submerged in sin and need.[166]

Edith would not see herself isolated in any way by her vocation to the hidden life of Carmel. To the contrary, she would exercise her vocation as a means to maintain a vibrant and dynamic spiritual connection with those in the world who are suffering and in so much need of prayer. Edith was convicted that "the deeper a soul is bound to God, the more completely surrendered to grace, the stronger will be its influence on the form of the church."[167]

I have a strong sense in my heart that Edith's influence on the Church and the world will continue to grow. I believe that she is calling us, not only to join her in prayer, but to continue her work, which is essentially the work of the Holy Spirit. She said that "all authentic prayer is prayer of the Church. Through every sincere prayer something happens in the

Church…for it is the Holy Spirit living in the Church that intercedes for every individual soul "with sighs too deep for words."[168] Together with that same Spirit, the communion of saints, and the special companionship of one in particular, our friend Edith Stein, women are being called from on high to renew the face of the earth through the example and offering of our authentic and surrendered feminine souls. It's an exciting mission!

LAST LESSONS

For all her worldly and spiritual achievements and intellectual brilliance, Edith's self-stated purpose and mission were quite simple: "If anyone comes to me, I want to lead them to Him."[169] And isn't that really what it is all about? This sentiment perfectly reflects the profound simplicity Edith gained through her loving spiritual surrender to Jesus. By grace, it is how she lived her life and how she embraced her death.

Her words elevate and empower, challenge and convict. Every time I contemplate them, I come away with a new level of understanding, a different insight or nugget of truth that speaks to my heart. Her example gives hope to all who are on a quest for truth. For as Pope John Paul II said at her canonization:

> At the beginning she devoted herself to *freedom*. For a long time Edith Stein was a seeker. Her mind never tired of searching and her heart always yearned for hope. She traveled the arduous path of philosophy with passionate enthusiasm. Eventually she was rewarded: she seized the truth. Or better: she was seized by it. Then she discovered that truth had a name: Jesus Christ.[170]

The legacy of Edith's love is unmistakable as she embraced the flames of martyrdom. Perhaps there is something beautifully poetic in her final recorded words, when she said, "*Give my love to the Sisters* [of St.

Magdalena]—*I am on my way to the East.*"[171] To the East, indeed, where the Son rises; to the East where she has found rest; and to the East from where the light of her beautiful feminine soul still shines in the open horizons of heaven! We are her sisters of today.

A New Beginning

My hope is that the end of this book is just a beginning for you, that it will serve both as an introduction and an invitation to delve more deeply into the life, thought, and heart of St. Teresa Benedicta of the Cross, our Edith Stein. I hope that sharing her thoughts and words with you has initiated a conversation of the heart that will sustain you on your journey as a Catholic woman and daughter of the King. My prayer is that you will let her wisdom seep into your feminine soul, as it continues to inform and inspire you to welcome the gifts of an authentic womanhood that is reflective of all the goodness and grace that God has to give you.

Join me now, won't you, in a quiet prayer of thanksgiving to God. It's a prayer to thank him for his infinite goodness, which has preserved the life and legacy of Edith Stein and enabled her to live on in the words she wrote and in the hearts of those who have come to know and love her through them. I hope by now you are one of those people!

Heavenly Father—we thank you for your beautiful daughter, Edith, our friend and saintly sister in Spirit, who so lovingly embraced all that you taught her, who received your cross with deep humility and joy, and who guides us still with the rich gifts of her wisdom and the fruit of her obedience. We are grateful for her example and her surrendered heart which only seeks to lead us to your Beloved Son.

*Father, help us to do your will above all things; to be the women
that you call us to be. Teach us to be ever grateful for the magnificent
mystery of our lives and show us how to welcome our dignity and
the dignity of every person.*

*Guide us by your Spirit to receive the beauty of our gifts and
attributes—the essential genius of our feminine souls.*

*And fill us every day with courage and zeal, in imitation of our
beloved Blessed Mother and through the intercession of our friend,
St. Edith, to express these gifts for the good of the world for your
greater glory—all for love for you. Amen.*

FINAL POINT TO PONDER

Millions of children today are homeless and orphaned, even
though they do have a home and a mother. They hunger for love
and eagerly await a guiding hand to draw them out of dirt and
misery into purity and light. Who else than our great holy mother
the Church should open her arms wide to take these beloved of
the Lord to her heart? But for this she needs human arms and
human hearts, maternal arms and maternal hearts.[172]

Will yours be one of them?

Costa, Anne. *Refresh Me, Lord! Meditations to Renew A Woman's Spirit.* Ijamsville, Md.: Word Among Us, 2008.

Garcia, Laura. "*Edith Stein—Convert, Nun, Martyr,*" *Crisis* 15, no.6. (June 1997).

Herbstrith, Waltraud. *Edith Stein: A Biography.* San Francisco: Ignatius, 1992.

Pope John Paul II. General Audience, 6 February, 1980. *Man and Woman: A Mutual Gift for Each Other.*

———. General Audience, 6 December, 1980. *Mary Sheds Light on Role of Women.*

———. General Audience, 16 January, 1980. *The Man-Person Becomes a Gift in the Freedom of Love.*

———. *Homily for the Canonization of Edith Stein.* Vatican City: 1998.

———. *Letter to Women.* Vatican City: 1995.

———. *Mulieris Dignitatem* (On the Dignity and Vocation of Women). Boston: Pauline, 1988.

Posselt, Teresia Renata, O.C.D. *Edith Stein: The Life of a Philosopher and Carmelite.* Edited by Susanne M. Batzdorff, Josephine Koeppel, O.C.D. and John Sullivan. Washington, D.C.: ICS, 2005.

Ratzinger, Cardinal Joseph, and Angelo Amato, S.D.B. *Letter to the Bishops of the Catholic Church on the Collaboration of Men and Women in the Church and in the World.* Vatican City: 2004.

Sharkey, Sarah Borden. "Edith Stein and John Paul II on Women," *Karol Wojtyla's Philosophical Legacy,* edited by Nancy Mardas Billias, Agnes B. Curry, and George F. McLean. Washington, D.C.: Council for Research in Values and Philosophy, 2008.

Stein, Edith. *Essays on Woman.* Translated by Freda Mary Oben, Ph.D. Washington, D.C.: ICS, 1996.

―――. *Edith Stein: Essential Writings.* Selected and edited by John Sullivan, O.C.D. Maryknoll, N.Y.: Orbis, 2002.

―――. *Life in a Jewish Family 1891–1916: An Autobiography.* Translated by Josephine Koeppel, O.C.D. Edited by Dr. L. Gelber and Romaeus Leuven, O.C.D. Washington, D.C.: ICS,1986.

―――. *The Hidden Life.* Translated by Waltraut Stein, PH.D. Edited by Dr. L. Gelber and Michael Linssen, O.C.D. Washington, D.C.: ICS, 1992.

―――. *The Science of the Cross.* Translated by Josephine Koeppel, O.C.D. Washington, D.C.: ICS, 2002.

Sweeney, Kathleen Curran. "Is There a Specifically Feminine Spirituality?" *Second Spring* 8, 2007.

Traflet, Dianne Marie. *Saint Edith Stein: A Spiritual Portrait.* Boston: Pauline, 2008.

Wilhelmsson, John, C. *The Transposition of Edith Stein: Her Contributions to Philosophy, Feminism and the Theology of the Body.* San Jose: Chaos to Order, 2012.

1. Waltraud Herbstrith, *Edith Stein: A Biography* (San Francisco: Ignatius, 1992), p. 110.

2. Herbstrith, *Edith Stein*, p. 94.

3. Herbstrith, *Edith Stein*, pp. 126, 129–130.

4. Herbstrith, *Edith Stein*, p. 133.

5. Edith Stein, *WOMAN*. Freda Mary Oben, PH.D., trans. (Washington, D.C.: ICS, 1996), p. vii.

6. John C. Wilhelmsson, *The Transposition of Edith Stein: Her Contributions to Philosophy, Feminism and the Theology of the Body* (San Jose: Chaos to Order, 2012), p. 101.

7. Wilhelmsson, *The Transposition of Edith Stein*, p. 102.

8. Dianne Marie Traflet, *Saint Edith Stein: A Spiritual Portrait* (Boston: Pauline, 2008), p. 5.

9. Herbstrith, *Edith Stein*, p. 20.

10. Edith Stein, *Life in a Jewish Family, 1891–1916: An Autobiography*. Josephine Koeppel, O.C.D., trans., Dr. L. Gelber and Romaeus Leuven, O.C.D., eds. (Washington, D.C.: ICS,1986), pp. 73–74.

11. Edith Stein, *Life in a Jewish Family, 1891–1916*, p. 74.

12. Edith Stein, *Life in a Jewish Family, 1891–1916*, p. 74.

13. Edith Stein, *Life in a Jewish Family, 1891–1916*, p. 77.

14. Edith Stein, *Life in a Jewish Family, 1891–1916*, p. 75.

15. Edith Stein, *Life in a Jewish Family, 1891–1916*, p. 138.

16. Edith Stein, *Essays on Woman*, p. 48.

17. Traflet, *Saint Edith Stein*, p. 8.

18. Edith Stein, *Life in a Jewish Family, 1891–1916*, p. 155.

19. Herbstrith, *Edith Stein*, p. 38.

20. Edith Stein, *Life in a Jewish Family, 1891–1916*, p. 260.

21. Edith Stein, *Life in a Jewish Family, 1861–1916*, p. 260.

22. Edith Stein, *Life in a Jewish Family, 1861–1916*, p. 401.

23. Herbstrith, *Edith Stein*, p. 51.

24. Traflet, *Saint Edith Stein*, p. 40.

25. Teresia Renata Posselt , O.C.D., *Edith Stein: The Life of a Philosopher and Carmelite*, ed. Susanne M. Batzdorff, Josephine Koppel, and John Sullivan (Washington, D.C.: ICS, 2005), pp. 59–60.

26. Edith Stein, *Life in a Jewish Family, 1891–1916*, p. 237.

27. Herbstrith, *Edith Stein*, p. 59.

28. John Sullivan, O.C.D, *Edith Stein: Essential Writings* (Maryknoll, N.Y.: Orbis, 2002), p. 37.

29. Posselt, *Edith Stein*, pp. 69–70.

30. Posselt, *Edith Stein*, pp. 67–68.

31. Herbstrith, *Edith Stein*, p. 88.

32. Edith Stein, *Essays on Woman,* p. 84.

33. Laura Garcia, "Edith Stein—Convert, Nun, Martyr." *Crisis* 15, no. 6, (June 1997), pp. 32–35.

34. Posselt, *Edith Stein*, p. 306.

35. Posselt, *Edith Stein*, p. 152.

36. Posselt, *Edith Stein*, p. 130.

37. Edith Stein, *The Science of the Cross*. Josephine Koeppel, O.C.D., trans. (Washington, D.C.: ICS, 2003), pp. xix.

38. Herbstrith, *Edith Stein*, p. 167.

39. Edith Stein, *The Science of the Cross*, pp. 32–33.

40. Traflet, *Saint Edith Stein*, pp. 133–134.

41. "The Marriage of the Lamb," September 14, 1940, in *The Hidden Life.* L. Gelber and Michael Linssen, eds., Waltraut Stein, trans. (Washington, D.C.: ICS), p. 100.

42. Herbstrith, *Edith Stein*, p. 181.

43. Herbstrith, *Edith Stein*, pp. 182–183.

44. Posselt, *Edith Stein*, p. 217.

45. Posselt, *Edith Stein*, p. 216.

46. John Paul II, "Homily of John Paul II for the Canonization of Edith Stein," October 11, 1998. Available at http://www.vatican.va/holy_father/ john_paul_ii/homilies/1998/documents/hf_jp-ii_hom_11101998_stein_ en.html.

47. "The Marriage of the Lamb," p. 100.

48. Edith Stein, *Essays on Woman*, p. 50.

49. Edith Stein, *Essays on Woman*, p. 87.

50. Kathleen Curran Sweeney, "Is There a Specifically Feminine Spirituality?: An Exploration of Edith Stein's Thesis" *Second Spring*, issue 8 (2007), p. 8.

51. Herbstrith, *Edith Stein*, p. 101.

52. Edith Stein, *Essays on Woman*, p. 56.

53. Edith Stein, *Essays on Woman*, p. 53.

54. Edith Stein, *Essays on Woman*, p. 53.

55. Edith Stein, *Essays on Woman*, p. 88.

56. Edith Stein, *Essays on Woman*, p. 143.

57. Edith Stein, *Essays on Woman*, p. 143.

58. Pope John Paul II, *Mulieris Dignitatem* (On the Dignity and Vocation of Women) (Boston: Pauline, 1988), pp. 101, 102. Emphasis in original.

59. Edith Stein, *Essays on Woman*, p. 47.

60. Edith Stein, *Essays on Woman*, p. 257. Emphasis in original.

61. Edith Stein, *Essays on Woman*, p. 107.

62. Sullivan, *Edith Stein: Essential Writings*, p. 112.

63. Edith Stein, *Essays on Woman*, p. 134.

64. Edith Stein, *Essays on Woman*, pp. 144–145.

65. Sullivan, *Edith Stein: Essential Writings*, pp. 64–65.

66. Edith Stein, *Essays on Woman*, p. 54.

67. Sullivan, *Edith Stein: Essential Writings*, p. 66.

68. Sullivan, *Edith Stein: Essential Writings*, p. 64.

69. Edith Stein, *Essays on Woman*, p. 119.

70. Sullivan, *Edith Stein: Essential Writings*, p. 63.

71. Edith Stein, *Essays on Woman*, p. 118.

72. Edith Stein, *Essays on Woman*, p. 135. Emphasis in original.

73. Edith Stein, *Essays on Woman*, p. 135.

74. Edith Stein, *Essays on Woman*, pp. 118–119.

75. Sullivan, *Edith Stein: Essential Writings*, p. 92.

76. Sullivan, *Edith Stein: Essential Writings*, pp. 138–139.

77. John Paul II, "The Man-Person Becomes a Gift in the Freedom of Love," General Audience, January 16, 1980, 2. Emphasis in original.

78. Edith Stein, *Essays on Woman*, p. 46.

79. Pope John Paul II, "Man and Woman: A Mutual Gift for Each Other," General Audience, February 6, 1980, 5.

80. Sweeney, "Is There a Specifically Feminine Spirituality?"

81. Pope John Paul II, *Mulieris Dignitatem*, p. 99.

82. Herbstrith, *Edith Stein*, p. 161.

83. Edith Stein, *Essays on Woman*, p. 70. Emphasis in original.

84. Pope John Paul II, *Mulieris Dignitatem*, p. 57.

85. Sullivan, *Edith Stein: Essential Writings*, p. 92.

86. Edith Stein, *Essays on Woman*, p. 136.

87. Edith Stein, *Essays on Woman*, p. 259.

88. Edith Stein, *Essays on Woman*, p. 45. Emphasis in original.

89. Edith Stein, *Essays on Woman*, p. 47. Emphasis in original.

90. Edith Stein, *Essays on Woman*, p. 95.

91. *Catechism of the Catholic Church* (Washington, D.C.: USCCB, 1994), 2370, quoting *Familiaris Consortio*, 32.

92. "Mission," Edith Stein Foundation, http://www.theedithsteinfoundation. com/about-2/mission/.

93. "Who Is Edith Stein?," Edith Stein Foundation, http://www. theedithsteinfoundation.com/about-2/who-is-edith-stein/.

94. Pope John Paul II, "Mary Sheds Light on Role of Women," General Audience, December 6, 1995, 1–2.

95. Pope John Paul II, *Mulieris Dignitatem*, pp. 56–57. Emphasis in original.

96. Edith Stein, *Essays on Woman*, p. 41. Emphasis in original.

97. Edith Stein, *Essays on Woman*, p. 97.

98. Edith Stein, *Essays on Woman*, p. 118.

99. Edith Stein, *Essays on Woman*, p. 109. Emphasis added.

100. Edith Stein, *Essays on Woman*, p. 62.

101. Edith Stein, *Essays on Woman*, p. 64.

102. Edith Stein, *Essays on Woman*, p. 49.

103. Edith Stein, *Essays on Woman*, p. 50.

104. Edith Stein, *Essays on Woman*, p. 50.

105. Sullivan, *Edith Stein: Essential Writings*, p. 37.

106. Edith Stein, *Essays on Woman*, p. 51.

107. Edith Stein, *Essays on Woman*, p. 51.

108. Edith Stein, *Essays on Woman*, p. 134. Emphasis in original.

109. Edith Stein, *Essays on Woman*, p. 134. Emphasis in original.

110. Edith Stein, *Essays on Woman*, pp. 53–54. Emphasis in original.

111. Edith Stein, *Essays on Woman*, p. 53.

112. Edith Stein, *Essays on Woman*, p. 96.

113. Edith Stein, *Essays on Woman*, p. 96.

114. Edith Stein, *Essays on Woman*, p. 102.

115. Edith Stein, *Essays on Woman*, p. 46.

116. Edith Stein, *Essays on Woman*, p. 255. Emphasis in original.

117. Sarah Borden Sharkey, "Edith Stein and John Paul II on Women," *Karol Wojtyla's Philosophical Legacy*, ed. Nancy Mardas Billias, Agner B. Curry, and George F. McLean (Washington, D.C.: Council for Research on Values and Philosophy, 2008), chapter twelve.

118. John Paul II, "Letter of Pope John Paul II to Women," 7, http://www.vatican.va/holy_father/john_paul_ii/letters/documents/hf_jp-ii_let_29061995_women_en.html.

119. Sarah Borden Sharkey, "Edith Stein and John Paul II on Women," Emphasis in original.

120. Edith Stein, *Essays on Woman*, pp. 96, 97.

121. Edith Stein, *Essays on Woman*, pp. 105–106.

122. Edith Stein, *Essays on Woman*, p. 74.

123. Adapted from Edith Stein, *Essays on Woman*, p. 75.

124. Edith Stein, *Essays on Woman*, p. 56.

125. Posselt, *Edith Stein*, p. 106.

126. Posselt, *Edith Stein*, p. 116.

127. Edith Stein, *Essays on Woman*, p. 120. Emphasis added.

128. Traflet, *Saint Edith Stein*, p. 83.

129. Edith Stein, *Essays on Woman*, p. 256. Emphasis in original.

130. John Paul II, "Letter of Pope John Paul II to Women," 9.

131. Cardinal Joseph Ratzinger and Angelo Amato, S.D.B., "Letter to the Bishops of the Catholic Church on the Collaboration of Men and Women in the Church and in the World," Offices of the Congregation for the Doctrine of the Faith, May 31, 2004, http://www.vatican.va/roman_curia/congregations/cfaith/documents/rc_con_cfaith_doc_20040731_collaboration_en.html.
132. Edith Stein, *Essays on Woman*, p. 266.
133. Edith Stein, *Essays on Woman*, pp. 266–267.
134. John Paul II, "Letter of Pope John Paul II to Women," 3.
135. Pope John Paul II, *Mulieris Dignitatem*, p. 9.
136. Edith Stein, *Essays on Woman*, p. 36.
137. John Paul II, "Letter of Pope John Paul II to Women," 10.
138. Edith Stein, *Essays on Woman*, pp. 240–241.
139. Edith Stein, *Essays on Woman*, p. 241.
140. Edith Stein, *Essays on Woman*, p. 241.
141. Traflet, *Saint Edith Stein*, p. 99.
142. Edith Stein, *Essays on Woman*, p. 260.
143. Edith Stein, *Essays on Woman*, p. 260.
144. Edith Stein, *Essays on Woman*, p. 260.
145. Pope John Paul II, *Mulieris Dignitatem*, pp. 65–66. Emphasis in original.
146. Traflet, *Saint Edith Stein*, p. 98.
147. Edith Stein, *Essays on Woman*, p. 264. Emphasis in original.
148. Katrina Zeno, "Why Woman?" Theology of the Body, http://www.theologyofthebody.net/index.php?option=com_content&task=view&id=76&Itemid=48.
149. Anne Costa, *Refresh Me Lord! Meditations to Renew a Woman's Spirit* (Ijamsville, Md.: Word Among Us, 2008), p. 58.
150. Posselt, *Edith Stein*, pp. 159–160.
151. Edith Stein, *Essays on Woman*, p. 84.
152. Sullivan, *Edith Stein: Essential Writings*, p. 64.
153. Edith Stein, *Essays on Woman*, pp. 267–268.
154. Edith Stein, *The Science of the Cross*, p. 162.
155. Edith Stein, *The Science of the Cross*, pp. 10–11.

156. "Teresa Benedict [sic] of the Cross Edith Stein (1891–1942): nun, Discalced Carmelite, martyr," Vatican, http://www.vatican.va/news_services/liturgy/saints/ns_lit_doc_19981011_edith_stein_en.html.

157. Pope Paul VI, *Evangelii Nuntiandi*, 18.

158. Pope John Paul II, *Ecclesia in America*, 73.

159. Edith Stein, *Essays on Woman*, p. 268.

160. Sullivan, *Edith Stein: Essential Writings*, p. 125.

161. Traflet, *Saint Edith Stein*, p. 139.

162. Sullivan, *Edith Stein: Essential Writings*, p. 130.

163. Sullivan, *Edith Stein: Essential Writings*, p. 129.

164. Sullivan, *Edith Stein: Essential Writings*, p. 129.

165. Sullivan, *Edith Stein: Essential Writings*, pp. 129–130.

166. Edith Stein, *The Hidden Life*, p. 29.

167. Edith Stein, *The Hidden Life*, p. 110.

168. Posselt, *Edith Stein*, p. 83.

169. "Teresa Benedict [sic] of the Cross Edith Stein."

170. John Paul II, "Homily of John Paul II for the Canonization of Edith Stein," 5.

171. Posselt, *Edith Stein*, p. 223.

172. Edith Stein, *Essays on Woman*, pp. 250–251.